A word about this series from
Toastmasters International

Who needs another book on public speaking, let alone a
series of them? After all, this is a skill best learned by practice
and "just doing it," you say.

True, but insight from people who've already been where
you are might help ease some bumps along the road and provide handy advice on handling stage fright and knotty
speech assignments.

After all, if practice is the best solution to public speaking
excellence, why is this country so full of speakers who can't
speak effectively? Consider politicians, business executives,
sales professionals, teachers, and clerics who often fail to
reach their audience because they make elementary mistakes,
such as speaking too fast or too long, failing to prepare ade-
quately, and forgetting to analyze their audiences.

Too often, we assume that because we try so hard to communicate, people will automatically understand us. Nothing
could be further from the truth! Listeners will judge us by
what they think we said, rather than what was intended or
even said. Simply put, the meaning of our message—and our
credibility—is determined by the reaction we get from other
people. The purpose of *The Essence of Public Speaking Series*,
then, is to help you in the communication process, prepare
you for the unexpected, warn you of the pitfalls, and, as a
result, ensure that the message you want to give is indeed the
same one people hear.

This series represents the accumulated wisdom of experts
in various speech-related fields. The books are written by
academically trained professionals who have spent decades
writing and delivering speeches, as well as training others.
The series covers the spectrum of speaking scenarios: writing
for the ear, using storytelling and humor, customizing particular topics for various audiences, motivating people to
action, using technology for presentations, and other important topics.

Whether you are an inexperienced or seasoned public
speaker, *The Essence of Public Speaking Series* belongs on your

bookshelf. Because no matter how good you are, there is always room for improvement. The key to becoming a more effective speaker is in your hands: Do you have the self-discipline to put into practice the techniques and advice outlined in these books?

I honestly believe that every person who truly wants to become a confident and eloquent public speaker can become one. Success or failure in this area solely depends on attitude. There is no such thing as a "hopeless case." So, if you want to enhance your personal and professional progress, I urge you to become a better public speaker by doing two things:

- Read these books.
- Get on your feet and practice what you've learned.

Terrence J. McCann
Executive Director, Toastmasters International

"This book is more than another how-to book in public speaking. It is a rare find. You will see your life experiences as an abundant resource of humor and stories. As a result it will enhance your speaking and enrich your life. Brilliant!"

> — Morgan McArthur, ATM, Toastmasters International 1994 World Champion of Public Speaking, veterinarian, professional speaker, dream-chaser

"Storytelling and humor lighten our load both as a speaker and listener. They open the heart, the mind, and the soul. Joanna Slan will show you how to touch your audience by making your speeches poignant, insightful, and humorous."

> — William Ecker, ATM, Toastmasters International Accredited Speaker, educatainer, trainer, and motivational speaker

"Joanna Slan can do it. It was obvious when she was a student that she could hold an audience, tell a story, make her point. Now, as a professional speaker, she has developed all those skills to a fine point. Even better, she has put it all in one place—her new book, Using Stories and Humor—Grab Your Audience. *As her former instructor, I'm using her suggestions in my own speaking!"*

> — Dr. Earl L. Conn, Dean, College of Communication, Information, and Media, Ball State University

"I stayed up 'way too late reading your storytelling book. It's incredible. This book reads like a pageturner novel. The fellow author in me can sense this book has been inside you for a long time. The relative ease that the information comes off of the page makes all of your ideas seem DOABLE."

> — Elaine Floyd, author, *Marketing with Newsletters*, National Speakers Association member

"*The real strength of* Using Stories and Humor—Grab Your Audience *is the down-to-earth practical insights to discovering and developing your personal story. This book should be in every speaker's library.*"

— Grady Jim Robinson, humorist, expert storyteller

Using Stories
and Humor

USING STORIES AND HUMOR—
Grab Your Audience!

JOANNA SLAN

WILLIAM D. THOMPSON
Series Editor

ALLYN AND BACON

Boston   London   Toronto   Sydney   Tokyo   Singapore

ISBN 0-205-26893-5

Printed in the United States of America
10 9 8 7   05 04 03

Text Credits:
pp. 70–71, reprinted with permission of Patricia Fripp; p. 99, reprinted
with permission of Mark Sanborn; pp. 149–150 reprinted with permission of the St. Louis Post-Dispatch, copyright 1996.

This book is dedicated to the
National Speakers Association (NSA),
particularly the Gateway (St. Louis) Chapter and
Professional Speakers of Illinois
(the Chicago chapter).
These speakers' love of life, desire to give of
themselves, and concern for members
have been a great source of joy in my life and
in the lives of countless other people.
I particularly want to thank
Patricia Fripp, for encouraging me to join NSA;
Patricia Ball, for her sterling
leadership and role modeling;
William Thompson, for his faith in me; and
Maggie Bedrosian, for her encouragement.

I also wish to thank Toastmasters, especially my
friends and fellow chapter members in St. Louis
and in Central Illinois. Their interest in
improving their stories and humor helped me
see the importance of my writing this book.

I would never have become a storyteller without
the willing ears of my family. I, therefore, wish
to thank my sisters Jane R. Campbell Newell and
Margaret W. Campbell-Hutts, who both listened
to my stories for years, and my husband David
and son Michael, who listen today.

Contents

How to Use This Book

Because, at their cores, storytelling and humor have so much in common, this book will be most helpful to you if you first go through the information on storytelling and then go on to humor. You'll soon see that humor represents a certain, stylized type of storytelling, and your understanding of the format and elements of stories will assist you in your attempts to be more humorous.

Throughout the book, you will find Tips, short blurbs of information that are tangential, but useful. Don't ignore them; they will accelerate your progress as a professional speaker.

At the end of each chapter is a short Summary. These give you the chance to review what you've learned and to make sure you haven't missed any important points; later they will serve as an easy way to review the content of each chapter.

Also at the end of each chapter are Exercises that encourage you to pursue what you've learned and to try out the new concepts you've encountered. If you are using this book in a study-group setting, the Exercises will give you guidance in putting the ideas into practice, as well as offer you a chance to discuss successes and problems further. In a classroom setting, the Exercises may help the teacher to make these abstract concepts more tangible.

This book will be most valuable to you if you see it as a jumping-off point. Let it encourage and guide you to find your own best, truest path as a storyteller and humorous speaker.

A History of Humans: A History of Storytelling

As the man hurried out and the door was shut, the Cardinal said, "Sit. You have a story to tell me."

Elizabeth Eyre, *Axe for an Abbott*

Tragedy brings forth the need to create meaning—to tell new stories—that can reweave the frayed ends of life into a coherent whole.

Joan Borysenko
Fire in the Belly

The old stories and the new stories with their old and new meanings enable us to purge our worries, tears, and sadness. We grow strong through them. They help us to know that we can be and are loved as well as liked.

Alida Gersie
Storytelling Magazine

HISTORIC PERSPECTIVE

Deep in a cave, silhouetted by the flickering fire against a damp wall, the storyteller mimics the lumbering gait of a large animal. Quickly, he shifts gears, and crouches behind a rock, contorting his face into a mask of fear. Now, he steps out from behind the rock and claps his hands together rapidly, echoing off the cave walls and creating a sound like that of a thundering herd. Again, he switches characters. He becomes the frightened hunter, awed and dwarfed by the stampede he sees before him. With great precision, the story-teller picks up a spear, runs, lunges, and jumps with joy into the air. Finally, he strides purposefully to the imaginary body of his kill and beams with pleasure.

His companions, huddled around the fire, turn to each other and smile. "That Ugg sure tells a mean tale, don't he?" (Remember: Grammar hadn't been invented yet!)

Of course, we can't be certain that cave people could talk, much less tell stories. But researchers are persuaded that early humans did communicate with each other. In two caverns in France, "where the cave art is dominated by horses, bison and other hoofed animals, a clapping noise gets echoed back and forth among the walls, producing a sound not unlike a stampede. Near the rear of the cave, however, where the images are dominated by panthers and other stealthy creatures, the walls reflect sound in such a way that it is muted," explains "The Dawn of Creativity," by William F. Allman (*U.S. News & World Report*, May 20, 1996). Surely, these puzzle pieces coupled with the stylized paintings speak to us as clearly as a modern tape recorder, sounding over the years, saying: "The urge to tell the stories of our lives has been with us since the birth of our existence."

What we do know is that humans have listened to—and struggled to record—stories in a variety of forms ever since our life on earth began. Nor are we humans alone in sharing stories. According to Jeffrey Moussaieff Mason and Susan McCarthy in their book *When Elephants Weep,* recordings of humpback whales show little variation in the songs they repeat from one year to the next. Researchers theorize the whales have an oral tradition. Mason and McCarthy write, "Perhaps they are telling the history of the species."

Because of mankind's desire to understand why we exist, our first stories grew from our religious beliefs. As far back as 3500 B.C., Sumerian poetry told the story of the death of Tammuz, son of the Mother Goddess Innin, while poetry in Babylonia described the creation of the world. Later, we puzzled over who we are. Between 700 and 600 B.C., Stesichorus of Sicily, the creator of the heroic ballad, began a tradition of singing great tales of great deeds. Finally, we bowed to the need to teach how we should live. One hundred years after Stesichorus, a former Phrygian slave named Aesop, told *fables,* quaint stories about animals with pointed lessons on right conduct.

At the heart of telling stories has always been the need to tell and to entertain. In Roman times, the wealthy paid singers to chant at banquets, strum instruments, and tell tales of the great gods, their loves, and their peccadilloes.

The best storytellers continue a long tradition of telling and entertaining. But no storyteller can be successful without a keen desire to meet the audience's needs.

One example of meeting the audience's needs comes to us from the colorful tarot cards widely available today for purchase. The tarot was first commissioned by nobility in the Middle Ages. But the illiterate masses quickly saw them as an aid for remembering stories gleaned from religious festivals. Lightweight, cheap, easy to transport and hide, the cards became the picture storybooks of the Middle Ages.

At other times in human history, stories were one way of keeping alive a culture when oppressors fought to extinguish it. Waves of conquerors in Ireland banished its native culture. If a person was caught wearing green or talking or writing Gaelic, the punishment was death. So the Irish preserved their traditions in the only way possible left to them: they told stories. Children huddled under the bushes alongside the roads and learned stories and songs about the history of Ireland—gatherings called hedge schools. Even today, the Irish so highly prize storytelling that one Irish businessman explained, "Storytelling is like a sport or an art form in Ireland." The art form even has its own name, *schalagging. Schalagging* happens when one person spins a yarn that takes in his unwitting listener. At the conclusion of the yarn, if the teller has been successful, he wins. It is then the obligation of the loser to try to fool the winner with a tall tale of his or her own. In this light-hearted way, the banter goes back and forth with the loser having been effectively *schalagged* by the winner.

As we enter the 21st century, technology has changed the ways we can deliver and access stories. Television has grown from small boxes of black-and-white images to color screens of nearly life-sized pictures. Radio and sound systems have improved so that the stories we hear in digitized code played over stereo units sound eerily like real life. Computers, fitted with compact disc players, allow us to interact and change the story on the screen. Headsets and images now create a virtual reality so precise that surgeons and pilots can be trained by them. Stories from around the world come to us in a flash via the Internet.

And yet . . . the most powerful tool of all remains accessible and largely unexplored. For the real joy of stories is the world they create within our minds. Without our brain's capacity to translate information, no stories would exist. Whether the mechanism is a computer, a television, or a human being standing alone on a stage, the true tale happens when a story engages the voice within our heads.

REMEMBERING THE ROLE OF STORIES IN YOUR LIFE

You have been surrounded by stories your entire life. Perhaps your earliest memory returns you to sitting on your mother's or father's lap and hearing "Goldilocks and the Three Bears." Or the "Three Little Pigs." Maybe—when you had to go to the bathroom the zillionth time before bedtime—a babysitter told you the story of the "Boy Who Cried Wolf."

In kindergarten, you sat with other children in a circle as the teacher read about ducklings crossing the Boston Public Gardens. As soon as you could read, you picked up fantastic stories from books. You met the cat in the hat and Harold with his purple crayon. From Sunday school at church or temple came the horrific tale of Daniel in the den of lions. And at Thanksgiving, with your family's bellies stuffed full, you begged your grandparents to share "the one about the time daddy set the garage on fire . . . ."

WHAT STORIES REALLY DO

A speaker was challenged by a participant in a training session. "How come you're wasting our time?" he snarled, his arms folded tightly across his chest. "What do all these stories have to do with our topic, communications? Why not cut the bull and tell us what we need to know?"

The speaker decided to ask the group for permission to continue. "All those who like hearing stories, raise your hands." About 95 percent of the room responded. The remaining stragglers admitted that they hadn't really thought about stories one way or the other. Mr. Grumpy slumped back in his chair and regressed into a catatonic state . . . until the goody cart showed up for the break.

What separates great presenters from mediocre ones are the stories. Time after time, a speaker who is invited to reappear before the same audience will be asked, "Are you going to tell us the story about the shampoo?" And another will pipe up, "And about the delivery drivers?" Brad Plumb, owner of The North American Speakers Bureau, Inc., has heard meeting planners whisper to speakers before a presentation, "Don't forget to tell them the one about . . . ." Plumb suggests that presenters are hired because the client "wants his group to hear a certain story that the speaker tells. The client wants to share the experience with the rest of the organization."

Dan Burrus, a technology futurist, explains, "What we have plenty of is information. What we need is wisdom." Stories translate information into wisdom by showing us the context in which we must view what we are learning.

Let's consider how you construct a presentation. You want a final product that can live and breathe and has a life of its own. So structurally, you will start with a skeleton composed of the outline of the presentation. The major bones of the skeleton are the points that need to be covered. The organs are the central themes of the presentation. But a skeleton by itself can't move around. Stories, then, are the muscles and cartilage that flesh out the skeleton and fill in all the empty spaces. The skin, which holds all the pieces together, is the delivery. The skin is crafted from body language and words and particular emphasis placed on the transitions you use to move smoothly from one topic to another.

Without stories, your pile of bones isn't going anywhere. It is a dry heap of clatter. The beauty of the body is the easy motion of the muscles, gliding and taking us from one place to another. So we remember the time we first rode our bike, a baby's first smile, the warm kiss of a lover. Stories are motion and emotion, and all that's worth remembering.

HOW STORIES WORK

Stories have existed from the dawn of mankind for a reason. "We understand everything in human life through stories," said Jean-Paul Sartre. All that we discuss, all that we think, all that we remember, comes to us through stories. The following are eight ways that stories work for us.

1. Stories Define Our Lives

Without stories, life would be a jumble of disconnected information. Instead, as actor and speaker Max Dixon explains, "Information plus emotion equals memory." Stories bring together the information and the emotional content of any given situation and allow us to shape the meaning. Perhaps you are late and are trying to apologize to your lunch date. How do you do that? You tell him or her a story about what happened to you. Or perhaps you were out with friends and something hilarious happened. You try to share it with another friend. So you tell the story. The story sequences the information, shapes it, and gives it meaning.

Although we think of stories as trivial, and we may have trouble remembering all the details of the stories we loved as children, stories can be stored within us on a cellular level, a level so deep and compelling that their presence may cause physical symptoms. A woman who recently attended her 25th high school reunion noticed the physical reaction she had to a schoolmate: "My stomach tensed and I felt nervous. But strangely enough, I can't remember why I feel that way. Obviously, my body remembers but my mind has lost the connection." What a shock it was for her to realize that our stories go so deep within us!

Because stories tell us who we are, the quality of our life is affected by the stories we tell ourselves. When people survive horrific events, their minds may react to the suffering by refusing to process and lay aside the trauma. This involuntary inability to move past the pain has been called post traumatic stress disorder (PTSD). Today, by using a new form of therapy called EMDR (Eye Movement Desensitization and Reprocessing), survivors can revisit the stories of their lives and create new interpretations. Thus, the woman who was once a rape victim can move from *I was violated and he took away my dignity* to *He did not take away my life and I showed great courage.*

EMDR works because we have a normal and natural desire to arrange information in stories, rather than in clumps of isolated facts. By rewriting our stories, we can come to peace with painful memories.

In fact, victims of various kinds of violence can regain control over their lives by retelling their stories. UCLA-based psychologist Shelley Taylor has found that the attempt to gain mastery over a traumatic event and over life in general separates those who recover from horrific misfortunes from those who do not. By honoring the deep level of their stories, victims access those disconnected memories and reshape them.

At every moment of life, we can see from only one vantage point. As ace trainer and adult-learning expert Sharon Bowman says, "The brain only lives in present time. Everything that happened to us—or that we imagined to have happened to us—happens in the present tense." When we rewrite a story, we change our present tense by changing the story. The new vantage point becomes our story, and our story becomes us. After all, who are you if you are not a sum of the stories you tell yourself about you?

2. Stories Organize Our World

The human brain constantly searches for patterns. Listen to jazz and you'll marvel at your mind's capacity to pick out the thread of a melody, no matter how the musicians turn that melody inside out and upside down. Drawing from the deepest beliefs of our culture, stories weave together complicated information, abstract ideas, and moral judgments.

In his book *Tell Me a Story*, artificial intelligence expert Roger C. Schank says, "People need to talk, to tell about what has happened to them, and they need to hear about what has happened to others, especially when the others are people they care about or who have had experiences relevant to the hearer's own life."

Another way to think of stories and their role comes from looking at the human brain as a computer. When we save information on a computer, we start by typing in seemingly random symbols which we must name and file for later use. Stories are one way we save information and store it for later retrieval.

3. Stories Allow Us to Learn

And yet **they protect us from consequence**, according to Norma J. Livo and Sandra A. Rietz in their book *Storytelling: Process & Practice*. They go on to explain, "We can learn from the literature without having to suffer the 'real' consequences, either inside the story or in our own real lives."

Although we can live but one life, through the magic of stories we can sample a thousand destinies. We can try to imagine being badly burned and then becoming paralyzed from the waist down, as did W Mitchell. We can try to imagine losing a 31-year-old spouse to a rare liver disease, as did Allen Klein. And we can try to imagine growing up the awkward son of a small-town football coach, as did Grady Jim Robinson.

As we share their stories, we take away new options for how we live. From the story of W Mitchell, we learn how to handle life's cruelest blows. W Mitchell never has a bad day. He has bad times, but not bad days. He asks himself what he has to do to change his mood and takes responsibility for his emotion. With Allen Klein's insights, we learn that "you can't stop the birds of sorrow from flying over your head, but you can stop them from making a nest in your hair." And, as Robinson tells us his poignant story of sibling rivalry, we too can appreciate his mother's wisdom as she encouraged him to quit comparing himself to his brother and start concentrating on his own unique talents.

Whatever befalls us in life, we have options. Way-showers who share their stories help us to see the choices we have, the lessons we can learn by reviewing the lives of others. As Robinson, a master storyteller and sage, says, "You can't hide the richest part of your life from the audience."

4. Stories Give Us a Way to Preserve What Matters to Us

Each time we tell a story, we rekindle a memory. The characters in the story come alive, for us and our audiences. Bureau owner Brad Plumb has often told his son, David, about the time young Brad hid under the family bed to light sparklers surreptitiously. Brad's ploy failed when the bed caught fire. Terrified by the blaze, Brad was unable to move. Smelling the smoke, Brad's mother raced into the bedroom and managed to lift both the wood-framed mattress and box springs off the bed frame so Brad could escape. After the blaze was out, the 95-pound Mrs. Plumb had to enlist the help of her two older sons to move the mattress and box spring again.

What David Plumb calls "the story about the time grandma morphed into Superwoman" satisfies many needs for the Plumbs. For Brad, the story brings to mind a picture of a woman so driven by mother-love that she was able to perform a feat of strength far beyond her normal capability. For David, the story offers a view of his father as a mischievous boy and of his grandmother as a family heroine.

By telling the story to his son, Brad has preserved and passed on a precious family memory. Each time we tell stories that matter to us, we honor our life experiences by keeping them polished as brightly as the family silver.

5. Stories Entertain Us While Stretching Our Mental Capacities

Many of the highest-paid people in our country are entertainers. The tedium and cares of our daily lives disappear, at least for a while, when we are being entertained. Modes of entertainment can be divided into passive and active. Television relies on passive involvement by the viewer. The viewer has only to sit before the magic box and a story unfolds before the couch potato's eyes.

By contrast, reading, playing music, and storytelling demand our active participation. Our brains must be switched to the "on" position to access these activities. Like any other muscle, if you don't use it, you lose it. When we read, play music, or hear a story, we engage our brains to process information. Thus, to hear a story, we must mentally construct the described scenes and characters and invite them to act out the situation on the stage within our brain. Now, your scenes and characters may not look exactly like mine, but they will be meaningful and relevant to you in a highly personal way.

Livo and Rietz explain that because stories follow conventional structures, the audience recognizes a story pattern. Because those patterns are mutually understood by the storyteller and the listener, "The audience can predict and control story shape during telling and participate directly in story construction." Hence, we see audience members lean over and whisper possible punch lines to each other, even when the story is new to them. Only one explanation exists for this whispered interaction: The audience was actively involved and, therefore, willing to predict an outcome.

6. Stories Promote Our Creativity

Creativity expert Sheila Glazov, author of *Princess Shayna's Invisible Visible Gift,* tells us, "Stories speak to the child in us,

the creative and curious person who never grows up. Listen
to any child and you'll hear the most marvelous and inven-
tive tales." When we were children, our minds were not fet-
tered by the word *impossible*. Because many stories have their
roots in the impossible, our minds are stretched and pulled in
dozens of new ways.

In his book *Tone Deaf and All Thumbs?* Frank R. Wilson
says, "A creative act must involve the communication of a
point of view, which is made possible because someone
moves, sees, compares, reflects, and then decides to let others
know about the experience."

All these motions take place when we are told a story. The
storyteller moves—and moves us. By means of vivid language, we "see." Internally, we compare our information and
life experiences to the story, and finally, we are invited to
reflect on what we hear.

7. Stories Help Us Feel Closer to Each Other

As Jim Harrison wrote in *The Legends of the Fall,* "We are so
largely unimaginable to each other." We exist as separate
beings in separate bodies living our separate lives. Deep
within, we crave an end to our loneliness. The desire to connect, to know and be known, leads us to tell our life stories to
perfect strangers in airplanes.

A *Star Trek* episode followed the exploits of an alien that
was pure, formless energy. In the final scenes of the program,
Mr. Spock, the Vulcan science officer, allowed the alien to
enter his body so that the being could experience "humanness." With awe and wonder, the being looked at his physical
form, looked at the others surrounding him, and noted how
terribly alone each person was. And so we are.

I do not know you. You do not know me. But when I
invite you to step into my story, we get to know each other.

When we tell stories from our lives and our experiences, we offer our life experiences to others. When you think about it, the goal of every artist is to offer his or her version of life to others.

By telling our stories, we allow ourselves to be real, human, and vulnerable in the presence of others. Robinson explains that "each person in your audience is connected to every other person in the audience, and to you, by a collective unconscious." This collective unconscious is shared with us by way of myths so that the effective speaker is one who transforms stories into larger themes which then transcend differences in geography, culture, social status, gender, and language.

8. Stories Help Us Develop a Sense of Humor

According to Marie L. Shedlock, author of *The Art of the Story-Teller,* stories help children develop a sense of humor "which is really a sense of proportion."

By helping us see our lives from another viewpoint, stories help us put life into a proper perspective. As Steve Allen says in *How to Be Funny,* "Given a little time for the pain to subside, dreadful experiences often can be the basis of funny jokes or stories." Grady Jim Robinson explains that humor is the other side of pain: "Humor happens when you have optimism. The audience sees you both as the victim and as triumphant because you are standing there telling the story and laughing. It is truly the touch of the divine." By seeing this happen in the lives of others, we can learn to apply this long-term view to our lives as well.

SUMMARY

Stories have been around since mankind first appeared on our planet. Stories perform eight vital functions:

1. Stories define our lives.
2. Stories organize our world.
3. Stories allow us to learn yet protect us from consequence.
4. Stories give us a way to preserve what matters to us.
5. Stories entertain us while stretching our mental capacities.
6. Stories promote our creativity.
7. Stories help us feel closer to each other.
8. Stories help us develop a sense of humor.

EXERCISES

1. Select a day to be a story detective. Listen to all the stories around you. Take notes about who is speaking and who is listening.
2. Revisit your childhood by going back and rediscovering your favorite stories from your youth. What did you like about those stories? Which one was your favorite? Where did you first hear the story?
3. For each of the eight vital functions of stories, give an example of a time when a story fulfilled that function for you.
4. Pretend you are a cave person. Create a story about your life. Tell it to someone else.
5. Share a story you have heard that helps you put life into perspective.

How Stories Affect the Listener

In my search for some illumination, I went back again to the myths to read them more carefully.

Rollo May, *The Courage to Create*

Storytelling works because there is a child in all of us, waiting for a good story to be told.

Bertram Minkin, quoted in the *St. Louis Post-Dispatch*

Storytelling is a basic part of every human culture—people have always had the need to participate emotionally in stories, and so the actor has probably played an important role in every society. But he should never forget that it is the audience that really does the work and is a pivotal part of the process.

Marlon Brando, *Brando: Songs My Mother Taught Me*

STORIES AND PROFESSIONAL SPEAKERS

Professional speakers are people who make their living giving oral presentations to audiences for the purpose of sharing knowledge and insight. Professional speakers are different from salespeople, who share information in order to sell a product. Professional speakers may work at presenting full-time, or they may speak in addition to other employment, and they may supplement their speaking with consulting, writing, and/or selling related products.

A trainer is a professional speaker whose responsibilities closely overlap those of a teacher. A trainer is hired when there is an expectation of specific skill transfer and when the class is expected to be highly interactive. Trainers and speakers do not evaluate (that is, grade) their audiences as teachers do. For our purposes, the terms *speaker* and *presenter* will be used interchangeably.

Two Types of Presenters

The scene is a lecture hall. The presenter walks to the lectern, adjusts the microphone, and begins to talk. You take notes as the speaker explains scientific findings discovered this year about the configuration of the eye of the fruit fly.

The scene is a banquet room. A presenter steps to the front of the stage and tells one side-splitting joke after another. You jot down a few punch lines to try in your office the next day.

You will feel quite different about these two situations. The first situation tapped the left, logical side of your brain. The presenter's style was not as important as the content. Therefore, this presentation was content-driven. Imparting information was the goal.

The second situation tapped the right, emotional side of your brain. The presenter's content was unimportant, but the style of delivery played a big part. Therefore, this presentation was emotion-driven. Entertaining the audience was the goal.

Of course, there is a place for both types of presentations in our world today. Of late, a great deal of emphasis has been placed on putting more content into speeches. At the same time, we live in a world of dazzle. With the proliferation of television stations, with the high quality of graphics on computer screens, and with the falling price of full-color printing, our audiences have come to expect that they will be entertained.

At a recent conference, an internationally known expert on women's issues gave a cogent, well-thought-out presentation. She was not flashy. She did not move around the stage or use her voice well. But she was a recognized expert in her field, and no one living knows more about the status of women in the United States than this woman. In another room at the same conference, a second woman spoke on a similar subject. The second woman did not cite any statistics or refer to any studies, but she did tell side-splitting tales of the problems men and women have relating to each other. The meeting planner was surprised that on the evaluations, listeners rated the expert as "boring" and the funny presenter as "wonderful." "That goes to show you," said the meeting planner, "delivery is everything."

To be fair, on occasion, content will supercede delivery. Take the computer programmer who is hired to teach a new computer language. The audience doesn't want to hear stories: it wants information. If the programmer slips in an amusing anecdote about the woman who tried to use her mouse as a pedal to run the computer, like the old-time sewing machines used a treadle, so much the better. But, in this scenario, any humor or storytelling will be a bonus and not an expectation.

Even if you have such a specialized expertise, remember: If all people wanted was content, they could go buy a book. If they are bringing you in, they want a human touch. And here's another reason giving a "book report" won't make for a good presentation. "Your statistics and facts can appear dated," says meeting professional Lynne Hellmer. Besides the Biennial Women's Conference, Hellmer is also responsible for staff-training sessions at the University of Illinois. "Your stories—if based on your personal life—have no date on them."

Hellmer has discovered that when she brings trainers into the university who concentrate on the research, they score very low on evaluations. Those trainers who offer a smattering of research and fill the rest of the presentation with stories score off the chart. And remember, this is at a university! These audiences earn a living dispensing academic excellence, often based on research. Yet, in a learning situation, their preference is . . . stories.

A schism has appeared in the speaking world between those who mandate content and those who offer "fluff." "Audiences demand fresh, updated content, the latest research!" one side bellows. "Stories and humor are just fluff!" Grady Jim Robinson acknowledges this fracture and says,

> I can think of no more important content than material that reflects and relates to the collective subconscious of all humanity. But, in spite of the life-changing potential of the personal story used as symbol to assist the listener through the continuing cultural paradigm shift, there will be meeting planners who insist on what they perceive to be content: data, numbers, studies, and research.

Obviously, the most powerful speakers will find a way to give the audience the best of both worlds: substance and sizzle. Jeanne Robertson explains: "You might use stories, humor, poems or music. But the professional speaker's fluff is what separates him or her from the non-professional." The most memorable and useful presentation will be the one that stimulates both sides of your brain—the logical fact-seeking side and the emotional experience-seeking side. Stories showcase content in an emotional setting. This two-pronged approach enhances both the initial attention your audience gives material and its long-term retention (see Figure 2.1).

Figure 2.1

DIAGRAM OF SIDES OF THE BRAIN AND TYPES OF PRESENTATIONS

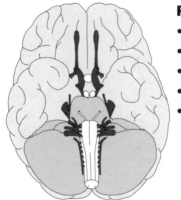

Left Brain
- Content
- "Steak"
- Words
- Conscious
- Linear
  Processing

Right Brain
- Emotion
- "Sizzle"
- Delivery
- Unconscious
- Wholistic
  Processing

WHY PROFESSIONAL SPEAKERS USE STORIES

Speakers use stories for a variety of reasons. The following section lists and explains five possible reasons.

1. Stories Get an Audience Listening

As Maggie Bedrosian says in *Speak Like a Pro,* "People listen well to stories—especially those with a lot of concrete, sensory detail." Audiences carry a lifelong positive association with stories.

At a recent convention, a female speaker told a story of her life focusing on one particular, life-changing incident. After a prolonged postpartum depression, the speaker was on her way to overcoming her inertia. She had found a hobby that interested her. She described her new-found joy of life, skillfully foreshadowing so that the audience realized her joy was to be temporary. The group sat motionless, silent, and hungry for every word. Then she shared her "bombshell." She explained that a knock on the door announced the accidental death of her spouse.

Standing in the back of the crowded room, one could see her impact on the audience. Almost as though a trap-door had opened in the floor, the crowd sank in their seats. The shock of her revelation became their emotional crisis as well.

Fortunately, you don't have to tell a story of life and death to get an audience's attention. A solid story well-told does not need to be of such consequence to be enthralling. But you will need to master the art of telling the story to get your best results.

2. Stories Offer Entertainment

Humans love to have a good time, which is why we pay entertainers more than we pay educators. In fact, think of how our economy would improve if the United States was as successful at exporting manufactured goods as we are entertainment.

Since the advent of cable television, the number of choices available to viewers has skyrocketed. Because we don't even need to leave our seats to change the channel, programs fight each other to offer higher levels of entertainment. Indeed, today's public speaker competes—at least in the audience's subconscious mind—not only with television and movies but also with music videos, computer animation, and CD-ROM devices on computers.

A speaker who does not offer stories may be hard pressed for a way to entertain the audience. Even if you play an instrument, do magic, or sing, how will you get a point across and fill an hour, if you don't tell stories?

The *American Heritage Dictionary* defines *entertaining* as "agreeably diverting, amusing." With the frantic pace of life and work pressures today, an audience needs its attention diverted. Otherwise, the message and value a speaker brings will go unheard.

3. Stories Provide a Change of Pace

Experts tell us that the longest an audience can sustain interest is 20 minutes, *unless* you offer a change of pace. Stories offer an effective way to change pace while continuing to drive home important information. If your presentation is shorter than 20 minutes, changes of pace guarantee a higher level of audience involvement and interest.

When planning the effective presentation, you will want to mix the emotional tones of your stories to achieve maximum impact. If all your stories harp on only one emotion, they will be perceived as being as monotonous as a test-tone on a television. The masters of gripping human drama often sprinkle in strategic humor to give the audience a chance to rebound from the intensity of the emotion. Otherwise, the audience may became overwhelmed, and may quickly "numb out": it may opt to quit listening rather than to feel the pain.

4. Stories Teach but Do Not Preach

Frequently, the professional speaker doubles as a human bandage. Organizations hire speakers "to fix a problem." As often happens on a personal level, organizations may vigorously deny the problems that plague them, and subsequently shoot the messenger who calls unwanted attention to those problems. Being a hired gun quits being fun about the time the troops fire on you with all barrels blasting.

The savvy speaker creates a safe space, much as a therapist does, for people to discover their problems—and cast about within themselves for the solutions to those problems. You can't do this by preaching from the platform.

Bringing an audience that delightful sense of discovery rewards both the speaker and the listeners. From the platform, there are few joys as sweet as seeing faces transform with new knowledge. Because the listeners have made this journey to discovery themselves, the insights received are highly personal. Personal insights imbued with enthusiasm create a powerful impetus to change.

For example, you can tell your audiences that taking the time to be with their children is important. You can cite statistics that show the average parent in the United States spends less than 13 minutes a day in one-to-one interaction with their kids. Or you can tell a story like this one of mine:

> I was awakened in the middle of the night by the phone ringing. No surprise—it was my dad. I was used to him calling me when he'd been drinking.
> "Sugar, sugar, I had a dream . . . "
> "What about, Daddy?"
> "I dreamed you and your sisters were little again. You were wearing those frilly pink dresses . . . and you had on those socks with the lace . . . and your shoes, your shoes were those black ones with the straps—do you remember, sugar? Do you?"
> "Yes, Daddy. I remember."
> "And you came running toward me, and I went to hug you, and I tried to hug you . . . but the minute I reached for you, you slipped through my hands . . . and . . . and . . . you were gone!" He sobbed into the phone. "What do you think it means, sugar? Oh, what can it mean?"
> "It means you missed your chance, Daddy."

Now, you tell me, which method of delivering the message "spend time with your kids" has more impact? Which one will you remember?

Stories trigger our natural impulse for comparison. True, a few listeners won't get it. But equally true, if the appropriate story skillfully sets up the right scenario, many listeners will get it, keep it, and run with it.

5. Stories Bond the Speaker and the Audience

Next time you see a movie, be an amateur sociologist. Note that while walking into the theater, attendees will barely speak to each other, much less hold open the door for each other. After the movie, the moviegoers will chat, help each other with coats, and hold open doors. What happened?

The crowd bonded.

When we share a story with a group of strangers, they have an experience in common: the story. More importantly for the speaker, the group now knows the speaker as a person because of what and how the speaker chose to share.

The minute a story hooks the crowd, the audience shares a new experience. Before the story, these people had nothing in common. Now, they know the same characters, feel the same feelings, and come to the same conclusions. A good storyteller weaves a powerful connective tissue in a time when people feel distanced from each other.

Besides bonding with each other, the moment the audience accepts the speaker's invitation to hear a story, it bonds with the speaker. Michael Klepper, author of *I'd Rather Die Than Give a Speech,* says, "The more you put yourself into your speech, the closer your heart is to the speech, the more your audience will be affected by it." Stories put our heart into speeches by putting our lives and our experiences out there for sharing. As Grady Jim Robinson says, "Human beings are touched on a universal level with stories. . . ."

Conversely, stealing someone else's material doesn't put *your* heart out there. Don't fool yourself by thinking you can get away with bogus material. Your audience may not realize you stole your material, but your presentation will still suffer because your body language and voice will betray your lack of credibility.

6. Stories Remind Us of Who We Are

For a world packed with people, we are curiously out of touch with each other. From the daily newspaper comes the story of a man who became angry at another driver who cut him off. The angry man reached under his seat and pulled out a gun, caught up to the other driver, and shot him through the head. We have all become such strangers to each other that we feel no responsibility toward each other. We are willing to take another's life to soothe our ruffled feathers because the other person means nothing to us.

Joan Borysenko, in a speech to the Professional Convention Management Association, noted,

> We live in a world where the intrinsic aspect of telling our story, of receiving one another, of creating meaning that is based on looking at the cycle of seasons, of sharing stories around the fire has been lost, and people, particularly North Americans . . . have ended up in the position of feeling isolated and separated in a way that we have never felt before in the history of the human race. What stresses human beings is the sense of isolation, separation, and the lack of meaning.

Stories bring us into each other's lives. When you share your story with me, you are no longer a stranger. When I tell you my story, from the platform, I remind you that we are much alike. In this simple way, we become human again. The gap between the speaker and the audience closes during a story.

7. Stories Enhance Memorability

"So, tell me about the speaker who talked to your group last year," said the speaker to the meeting planner and members of her meeting committee.

Each committee member agreed that last year's speaker had been excellent. But, to a person, no one could remember last year's speaker's name. Finally, in an attempt to tease the missing name from her friends, a committee member remembered that last year's speaker told a hilarious story about her son and a piece of candy.

Last year's speaker was, of course, Karyn Buxman.

When your stories are uniquely yours, your name will eventually surface with the tale. Long after they forget our names, they remember our stories. Long after they forget the points we tried to make, they remember our stories. That's all we need to know: The audience remembers stories.

WHY STORIES ARE SO IMPORTANT TO THE PROFESSIONAL SPEAKER

Ace meeting planner Lynne Hellmer has observed firsthand the impact stories have on an audience. Hellmer plans the University of Illinois Biennial Conference for Working Women, the largest conference of its kind in the country. Watching the audience carefully, she notes that an observer can tell when a story is beginning by the changing body language of the audience. "The bodies relax and their eyes light up," says Hellmer.

Stories return us to a childhood state of accepting consciousness, called a "sacred space." This space exists where the head and the heart connect. A speaker invites the audience into this sacred space in order to share the deepest truths we have to offer. We share these truths without pretense or arti-fice, on a deeply personal level, and the audience knows it.

The audience, in return, listens without a critical ear. It suspends its cynicism and allows the story to penetrate its consciousness. A curious transformation happens: The story no longer belongs to the speaker but becomes the property of the listener. Our minds do not distinguish between what we have experienced in real life and what we have experienced vicariously. If I tell you I am sucking on a juicy, yellow lemon, and that the tart liquid is causing my mouth to pucker up, your mouth begins to salivate. Thus, our lives meld with the lives of the audience when we tell stories.

Without authenticity, this never happens. With passion and congruity, it simply must happen. The end result is, as Grady Jim Robinson explains, "A listener is invited, but not forced into potentially different ways of seeing things."

In sum, the best speakers are the best storytellers. The best speakers will entertain, invite, and entice their listeners into a world where new ideas can be examined, approved, and adopted. Whether the speech is serious or humorous doesn't matter: The delivery of the message is enhanced with stories because stories help us reach our deepest level of understanding.

Stories support points by giving information context. Without context, information exists only as clutter. If you were told, "63, 118, 43," you would not know whether you were being given my measurements or the combination to my locker—until that information is given context. When the professional speaker combines context and information, the resulting format allows the audience to interpret instantly what is said in a holistic manner. In *Tell Me a Story,* Roger C. Schank explains that "storytelling and understanding are functionally the same thing."

By nature, human beings tend to match new information offered with information preexisting in our minds. Communication experts call this phenomenon "disclosure matching." Gerald R. Goodman, in *The Talk Book,* explains that disclosure matching "is the bedrock stuff for the making of any long-term association or relationship." When a speaker tells a story that actively involves the audience, the audience members internally match that story to their personal experiences. If the story is a good match, the audience members quickly, mentally run to their personal story repositories in their own brains and check out similar stories.

We all file our stories differently. Therefore, if one person hears a story about a boy and his dog, she might run to her personal shelf marked "boy" and you might run to your shelf marked "dog." The more places we can find a similar story, the better the chance the story will be remembered—because we will file this new story alongside our previously existing one. So, a story that can be filed under "dog," "boy," "summer," "Indiana," "vacation," and "fleas" will afford the listener many filing options. As Schank explains it, ". . . Thinking involves indexing. . . . The more information we are provided with about a situation, the more places we can attach it to in memory and the more ways it can be compared with other cases in memory. Thus, a story is useful because it comes with many indices."

HOW PROFESSIONAL SPEAKERS USE STORIES

The stories you hear from professionals on the platform will stand time's test if they are true, universal, and well-thought-out. No, you won't hear of dragons or fairies or elves, but listening to the great speakers of our time, you will hear of human feats of courage, self-discipline, and determination. Even the more mundane stories of everyday life have value, as they remind us that we are not alone in our daily toils, but rather, we are part of a universe of people trying and failing and going on in a thousand personal endeavors.

Modern professional speakers can rightly take their places as the storytellers and mythmakers of our times. The body of work developed by professional speakers will provide important references to the concerns of our culture and times for years to come. While a professional speaker might make reference to any of the traditional story forms that we will discuss later, the majority of professional speakers rely heavily on a variation of the anecdote called the personal anecdote and on personal vignettes. For the sake of simplicity, we will call both by the term *stories*.

Stories may be poignant, insightful, humorous, or all three. In Chapters 9, 10, and 11, we will discuss humor in depth. Until then, keep in mind that for the professional speaker, humor exists as a variation of stories in general. Or as Robinson explains, "Humor and storytelling for the professional speaker go hand in hand."

Typically a speaker will use a story in one of three ways. These uses are described on the following pages.

1. The Speech as a Story

In this situation, the speaker's entire presentation works as a story. The presentation is obviously staged and scripted. If you were to hear this presentation from this speaker in more than one venue, you would hear essentially the same presentation almost word for word. Even if a few minor words change here and there, the basic premises, the transitions, and the overall wording of the points and anecdotes won't.

To prepare for this type of presentation, the speaker has probably dictated it word for word and then memorized the edited result. For a speaker who presents in this manner, the greatest challenge is appearing to be spontaneous despite the fact that the presentation has been carefully worded and choreographed.

The benefit of a presentation as a story lies in its perfection and its low level of risk. By working and reworking material and by sticking closely to the script, a speaker rarely wanders into risky territory. For many meeting planners, knowing that a speaker's presentation has been practiced and given countless times assures them that they are buying a proven product. On the flip side, these presenters can come across as stiff and wooden. Because the presentation is so blatantly a show, an audience has to decide whether to join in or to opt out. And because the presentation is so tightly choreographed, a misstep can be fatal. For example, if anything causes the audience to feel animosity toward the speaker, the speaker has limited options—because the speaker and the script are joined at the hip. What can go wrong? A fire alarm, a disastrous annual report, a last-minute presentation that was not in the plans by someone asked to say a few words, or an excess of liquor can all wreak havoc with the presentation the speaker planned to give.

This is what happened to a speaker who was hired to speak to a group of home builders at an after-dinner banquet. The night of the banquet, the sky poured so much rain that the speaker could easily conceptualize Niagara Falls. The home builders sloshed through the door one by one. Tired, wet, and hungry, they first headed for the open bar that a local lumberyard had sponsored. The meal was pushed back an hour. (This is always a BAD SIGN. Write that down. If it happens to you, begin to panic early.) The sponsoring lumberyard graciously announced that they were going to leave the bar open all night. Everyone finally sat down to dinner. The speaker turned to shake hands with the man seated to her left, a gentleman who smiled and said, "Hi, I'm tonight's guest speaker."(A second BAD SIGN. At this point, you should run to the bathroom and check your copy of the contract.) Turns out, the gentleman was from the Chamber of Commerce and had been asked to say a few words. He got up and explained that the Chamber was really worried about infrastructure in this fair city. As the speaker mulled over what *infrastructure* meant, the Chamber executive made his meaning perfectly clear: "For example, I took a call on my cell phone right as dinner was served. Two major subdivisions in our city have been caught in a flash flood."

Now, did those men want to hear the scheduled presentation? No. They wanted to know if their building sites were flooded. The crowd rose as one and ran to the phones. Hearing the worst possible news, they shrugged sanguinely and ordered more beer, thank you very much.

By the time the contracted, scheduled speaker was introduced, half the builders had checked out physically and the other half had checked out mentally. In fact, the only people feeling pain were the meeting planner and the speaker. (This was the third BAD SIGN. But, remember, a contract is a contract, and if the client says, "I still want you to speak," you do it. And the speaker did.)

2. Stories Appear "Spontaneously" to the Speaker

In this shape of a presentation, the speaker appears to be engaging the audience in a conversation. Along the way, the speaker seems to remember stories that support ideas.

This style of speaking has much more risk involved than the choreographed speech does. Often, a speaker who works this way will have a general idea of what he or she wants to cover and then . . . well, he just sort of wings it. As one speaker explained to me, "I have a filing cabinet in my mind. I don't know what I'm going to say until I say it. As the presentation rolls on, I just open that filing cabinet and reach in and pull out what I think will fit."

Lest this seem too spontaneous, please note: Usually, this type of speaker has spoken extensively and has used these anecdotes before. However, the shape of the presentation and what gets included may change dramatically depending on the speaker's mood and the venue.

Meeting planners like this kind of speaker because the feel is less staged and more real. The entire presentation can, if done well, come across as warm and engaging. On the down side, speakers who work like this risk a lot. You can go blank, you can choose the wrong anecdote, and you can misjudge time. To counter the problems associated with this spontaneity, some speakers use preselected slides or overheads to guide them through the presentation, prompting them to tell rehearsed stories. By watching an inconspicuous clock, or by using a vibrating pocket-sized timer, a speaker can keep track of time, expanding or contracting the number of stories as needed.

3. Stories Are Told in the Storytelling Tradition

This type of presentation represents a hybrid. Here, the speaker tells the story, setting it apart the way a gem is set in a ring. Audiences know immediately when the speaker has become a storyteller. Audiences suspend their belief, for a few moments, and listen as children listen when they are told a story. An unspoken agreement must ensue—"I'm telling this and you are going to be polite and listen." This part of the presentation may stand alone or the story may be one of a sequence of stories. Usually, after the story, the presenter will "debrief" the audience by discussing the import of the story.

The rest of the presentation may be given conversationally or in a choreographed manner. Typically, it would be given conversationally with an invitation to the audience to share its interpretations of the story.

A variation of this is to act out the story, thus creating a vignette within a speech. This can be done on a variety of levels. Simply inclining the head, adding a slight vocal change, or changing position on stage offers one simple way to act out a story. Another would be to actually "act" by assuming a variety of characters.

Done with dramatic talent, this offers yet another way of introducing variety into a speech. Patricia Ball, 1996 president of the National Speakers Association, uses her background as an actor to create dramatic vignettes within her presentations. Ball deftly introduces the story and the character and then acts out all the parts. By changing her voice, her mannerisms, and her position on stage, she becomes a child, a historic figure, or a harried secretary. The effect mesmerizes her audiences.

AND WHY STORIES ARE EVEN MORE IMPORTANT TO THE "NONPROFESSIONAL" SPEAKER

What about the "nonprofessional" speaker? The person who speaks only occasionally and doesn't make a living from the platform?

Stories are even more important to this group because adding stories will quickly add polish and interest to presentations. Without stories, presentations begin to sound like book reports. For the nonprofessional, stories are a critically important way to win and hold the attention of an audience.

Occasional speakers may shy away from sharing about themselves because they will think it unprofessional. What a mistake! Stories move audiences. If getting results is the goal, stories will accomplish the job better than dry recitations of facts ever could.

A woman reported this storytelling episode, which happened to her and her boss. They both worked for a government housing agency. The agency was asked to make a presentation to the local Chamber of Commerce. Her boss went first, citing the numbers of houses financed by his agency. He cited the agency's mission statement. He went on and on, reciting number after number. Then he sat down. During her turn to speak, the woman shared this story:

> When I was seven, my grandmother came to live with us. She was unable to live by herself because her house had stairs and no handrails. Grandma's temperament was never gentle, and the loss of her privacy, the noise of us children, and the lack of familiar surroundings heightened her naturally cranky disposition. What I remember of my childhood is this: My angry grandmother, my depressed mother, and my father leaving the house each evening for any and every excuse he could find. By the time my grandmother died, our family was in ruins.
>
> Our rural housing program for the elderly could have helped Grandma stay at home. I urge you to direct families to us as a resource.

And with that, she sat down.

Afterward, the woman was engulfed by business people who thanked her for her presentation. "Now, I see," said one businessman, "why your agency is so valuable. I, too, remember having the grandparents move in with us. It was a nightmare."

In a corner, her boss stood alone fingering his brochures and handouts.

If a presentation is worth your time to tell it, and the audience's time to listen, it's worth pulling out all the stops and aiming for maximum impact. Remember: Stories get results.

SUMMARY

The better the professional speaker, the more likely that he or she tells terrific stories. Stories keep audiences listening, entertain, change the pace, teach but do not preach, and create a bond between the presenter and the audience while reminding us who we are and enhancing the memorability of the message. Speakers use stories in a variety of ways. Even those who do not speak "professionally" can use stories to improve the impact of their messages.

EXERCISES

1. Watch an audience respond as a speaker tells a story. Make notes about the physical changes you notice.
2. Ask a person to tell you and a friend a story. Now, write down all the ways you might index that story.
3. Interview three people about the ways they might use stories in their jobs and in their lives.
4. Listen to a professional speaker and a nonprofessional speaker make presentations. Who uses more stories? What is the impact of the stories?
5. Prepare a presentation on a technical topic. What stories could you use to enhance the presentation? (Technical topics include computing, car maintenance, health care issues, use of cosmetics, a how-to demonstration, and a sales pitch.)

Types of Stories and Their Use by Professional Speakers

Nothing in recent years, on television or anywhere else, has improved on a good story that begins "Once upon a time . . . "

William J. Bennett, *The Children's Book of Virtues*

People are hungry for stories. It's part of our very being. Story-telling is a form of history, of immortality too. It goes from one generation to another.

Studs Terkel, oral historian

And the draw of all the various sorts of stories, magical and mundane, can't be explained as our interest in simple problem solving. Every good story does involve sympathetic, interesting characters facing some form of problem, either with self, others, nature or God. But mere problem solving would get tiring after a while.

Douglas Jones, *Agenda*

We both love using really good stories to illustrate points in our seminars.

Jack Canfield, talking about how he and coauthor Mark Victor Hansen came to compile their *Chicken Soup for the Soul* books, *People* magazine

TYPES OF STORIES

Stories differ by length, type of characters, deeds, and purpose. While professional speakers rely primarily on anecdotes, a working knowledge of all kinds of stories assists a professional speaker in crafting his or her own stories. In addition, we can practice our delivery of stories with these time-tested tales. All stories share a common anatomy, just as all mammals have hair, are warm blooded, and suckle their young. All stories feature a mix of characters, action, crisis, and resolution.

Pulitzer Prize winning author Jon Franklin defines stories this way: A story consists of a sequence of actions that occur when a sympathetic character encounters a complicating situation that he confronts and solves.

The following section lists and defines the common types of stories.

Parable

A *parable* is a short story of an everyday deed told to illustrate a religious teaching using people as characters. Example: The widow's mite. In the New Testament, Jesus illustrates that the amount we give is not as important as the proportion of the sacrifice we are making. He does this by comparing the large amount given to the temple by the wealthy to the small amount—the mite—given by a widow.

Fable

A *fable* is a short story of an everyday deed told to teach a moral value using animals as characters. Example: "The Tortoise and the Hare." Aesop tells us that "slow and steady wins the race" by contrasting the overconfident hare to the dependable tortoise.

Fairy Tale

A *fairy tale* is a short- to medium-length story told to entertain using supernatural creatures (such as fairies, gnomes, dragons, and witches) and humans as characters. Example: "Cinderella." A fairy godmother saves Cinderella from a life of never-ending drudgery by dressing her appropriately and sending her off to the ball.

Myth

A *myth* is a short- to medium-length story told to explain natural phenomena and used as a religious guide using superhumans and humans as characters. The characters are archetypal, which means they hark back to original characters who appear over and over in stories. The wicked stepmother, the brave hero, and the faithful friend are all archetypes. Example: "Jason and the Golden Fleece." Although Jason was heir to the throne of Iolcus, his uncle reigned as king. To win back the throne, Jason had to bring home a Golden Fleece guarded by a never-sleeping dragon. After many adventures, with the help of the lovely young sorceress Medea, Jason snatched the fleece.

Anecdote

An *anecdote* is a short story drawn from everyday life told to entertain, enlighten, and educate using humans as characters. Anecdotes are frequently humorous or pointed. Example: "I'll drive around and pick you up," said the husband to his wife. She raced out of the car into the rain to run her grocery store errand. After paying for her purchase, with her head down, she ran back out into the rain and threw herself into the car waiting outside the entrance. Her skirt was hiked around her thighs. Rain was streaming from her hair. She glanced to her left and saw the astonished expression on the face of a stranger. "Why, Charlie," she said breathlessly, "You've grown hair!" Her response reminds us that often we add 2 and 2 and wind up with 40 instead of 4!

Personal Anecdote

A *personal anecdote* is a term used to distinguish a story told by the speaker about the speaker. Van Cliburn tells of receiving a picture book as a child for Christmas. Eagerly opening the book, he flipped to a picture of the Church of St. Basil in Moscow. "Oh," he said to his parents, "Can we go see this?" Like all good parents, they smiled down at him and said, "Maybe, Sonny, someday." When Van arrived in Moscow, he asked immediately if he could go see the Church of St. Basil. "It was all lit up with these little lights. Snow was whirling all around. People asked if I was nervous [about the Tchaikovsky International Piano and Violin Festival] and all I could think was how happy I was to be there."

Folk Tale

A *folk tale* is a fantasy of unknown origin told to explain a natural phenomenon or occurrence. The cast of characters includes humans and creatures. While a folk tale may be unique to a particular culture, variations of the tale may crop up in many cultures. Example: Rudyard Kipling's *The Jungle Books*. From the these books came Disney's movie *The Jungle Book,* the story of Mowgli, an orphan who is raised by wolves in the jungle.

Tall Tale

A *tall tale* is a short story based on exaggerated human characters from everyday life told to entertain and to explain natural phenomena. Example: Paul Bunyan. Paul Bunyan was a larger-than-life lumberjack who cut down trees in the north-western United States.

Bit or an Exercise

A *bit* or an *exercise* is a nonstory story having the same dramatic appeal of a story. The bit uses the audience as characters by asking them to take part in the presentation. The speaker structures a situation that involves the audience, which produces the story. For example, Rebecca Morgan asks audience members to mingle with each other and touch each other on the nose. This has no plot, but the exercise creates a plot by involving characters (the audience members) in action (the mingling and nose touching) which results in a climactic experience ("I can't believe I touched my CEO's nose!"). Morgan then uses the experience as a teaching tool, thus helping the group process the situation.

Chestnut

A *chestnut* is an anecdote so frequently retold that the origination is lost. Lilly Walters defines chestnuts as "stories, jokes, or songs that have been overused and are stale."

Vignette

A *vignette* is a slice-of-life story drawn from everyday life told using humans as characters to evoke a mood. Mood is paramount in the vignette, and it may have little action or plot. Example: Sheila Murray Bethel talks of taking an early-morning cab ride each time she visits Washington, DC, so that she has the chance to visit the Vietnam Veteran's Memorial.

One-Liner

While often thought of as a joke, a *one-liner* can be the result of boiling down any story to its most basic premise or punch line. One-liners are often overlooked because they are deceptively simple, and yet they can speak volumes. Business-owner Maurice Fox explained the history of an enormous white house set like a jewel in a well-tended yard along the Battery, a famous historic district in Charleston, South Carolina. "When I was a child," said Fox quietly, "there was a sign in the yard of this house that said, 'No dogs or Jews allowed.'" That simple, single line tells an entire story of what it was like to grow up Jewish in Charleston in the 1940s.

A one-liner can be set up by the speaker to create a "golden thread" which can next be "pulled through" the entire garment of a presentation. One speaker who has mastered this technique is Emery Austin. She begins her presentation by setting up the phrase, "What would an extraordinary person do under these circumstances?" Then, moving from one scenario to another, she repeats the one-liner. By continually bringing the audience back to that phrase, she zeroes in on the visionary nature of the words.

In another way, a one-liner serves as a sort of cultural shorthand to describe a larger, more complex situation. So, when a colleague complains about the success of another colleague, we might be moved to say, "That's sour grapes." The term *sour grapes* came from an Aesop's fable in which a hungry fox jumped and jumped to reach grapes hanging from a vine in a tree. Finally, disappointed by his failure to reach the grapes, the fox walks away, muttering to himself, "They were probably sour."

Many times, we rely on one-liners to share both information and mood quickly. The term *sour grapes* conveys a mood of petty dismissal. When we hear it, we know that the person complaining is merely consoling him- or herself and does not really believe the desired object to be worthless. Obviously, the more you know about the origin of these one-liners, the better you can use them. Knowing what educated Americans know has been called *cultural literacy,* a term coined by E. D. Hirsch, Jr. The difference between a culturally literate speaker and an illiterate one parallels the difference between an artist who has a box of 96 crayons and one who has a box of 8. Certainly, you can create a beautiful picture with 8 crayons, but obviously you have more possibilities when you can work with 96 different colors.

To become a great speaker, you need lots of crayons. Then you can color pictures that appeal to all sorts of audiences. You can become more culturally literate by reading, exposing yourself to new experiences, and maintaining a vivid sense of curiosity.

USING THE DIFFERENT TYPES OF STORIES

All the different types of stories listed can be used skillfully if speakers take time to match the form and the message appropriately to the audience. Trainer Sharon Bowman, author of *Presenting with Pizzazz! Terrific Tips for Topnotch Trainers!,* stresses that adults will usually go along with your requests if you first tell them why you have chosen a specific activity. So, if you choose to tell fairy tales to an adult audience, you would want to put the fairy tales in a context that would make them meaningful to the adults. You might say,

> Today we're going to talk about the effect of positive and negative communication on our lives. To illustrate how communications styles can have impact, I'd like to tell you the story of "Rumpelstiltskin." This is a fairy tale about an evil gnome who demands that the princess must guess his name or give up her newborn baby to him. Eventually the gnome's bragging leads to

the discovery of his name. In other words, his negative communication style was his downfall.

In the same manner, you can use any type of story to illustrate a point—as long as the relationship between the story and the point is made clear. Certain types of stories will be more appropriate and more compelling for certain groups. By learning all you can about your audience, you can pick and choose the type of story and match it carefully to the needs of the listeners.

Looking for patterns within gives us another way to use the different types of stories. The pattern of "Goldilocks and the Three Bears" can be repeated to show job seekers how one challenge may be too big, one challenge may be too small, and one may be just right.

Think about learning stories that exist in literature as just like learning to play scales on a musical instrument. By repeating scales, the musician develops technical expertise and the ability to forecast which notes will appear in a sequence. Similarly, classical stories can teach you plotting techniques that will allow you to craft a situation having both conflict and a satisfying resolution.

CLASSICAL STORYTELLING

Storytelling employed by professional speakers and the kind of storytelling that exists today as an outgrowth of an ancient art are distinctly different.

In 1915, a French woman named Marie L. Shedlock published the first American edition of *The Art of the Story-Teller,* about an art which she defined as "almost the oldest art in the world—the last conscious form of literary communication." Her book signaled a renewed, formal interest in the ancient art that had been passed along by itinerant tale spinners. Shedlock systematically dissected an art form to narrow the gap between those who were naturally gifted and those who were not.

Classical storytelling sprang from the roots of dramatic narratives, a type of one-person play. (Although we take for granted the appearance of a troupe of actors in plays, they were historically performed by one person. Aeschylus introduced a second actor in 471 B.C., and Sophocles introduced a third actor in 468 B.C. Think of the debt the actors' union and Hollywood owe these two men!)

To be an effective storyteller, the tale spinner acts out all the elements of the story. Stories for classical storytelling come from literature and from folk tales preserved through oral history. The storyteller is not usually the creator of the story. Typically, the story is memorized and repeated verbatim—or nearly so—at each telling. Gestures and vocal emphasis are stylized and, on occasion, charted for memorization along with the script of the story. Much of the time, the intended audience is children.

Classical storytelling builds drama through plot, dramatic interpretation, and expectation. Frequently, repetition creates a harmony within the story, developing a cadence and a sense of expectation. In the story "The Three Little Pigs," repeating the phrase, "Or I'll huff and I'll puff and I'll blow your house down!" elicits loud squeals of joy from children as they echo the phrase along with the storyteller.

The elements of classical storytelling prove useful on the platform and studying these elements has great value to the professional speaker. In fact, so powerful is storytelling from the platform that two speakers, Jack Canfield and Mark Victor Hansen, have founded a dynasty with their *Chicken Soup for the Soul* books, which all feature 101 stories. These books have commanded the top spots on the *New York Times* self-help bestseller lists with sales at this writing of 3.1 million copies.

Because of our growing recognition as a society of story-telling's value, efforts have been made to codify stories often told by tale spinners. These stories frequently give us extraordinary insight into a culture and its values. By recording these tales, we preserve cultures that may be in danger of disappearing.

One woman who has done this is Nancy Rhyne, whose books *Tales of the South Carolina Low Country* and *More Tales of the South Carolina Low Country* preserve the stories of South Carolina, which, according to archivists at the Library of Congress, "is richer in folklore than any other state." Rhyne traveled through the state interviewing millionaires and humble folks to compile her tales.

Rhyne's stories help preserve the culture of the slaves who came to the South Carolina coast and spoke an African-English patois. She explains that "over the generations, the original dialect was mixed with French variations and gave way to a slaveese called Gullah."

> These are the stories I heard growing up, as told by my South Carolinian grandmother as she rocked back and forth in the wide-slatted rocker on her piazza in Summerville, South Carolina. Her favorite Gullah story went like this: At a bus stop, a old woman stepped on. The bus driver looked over and said, "Hey, Auntie, you can't get on de bus with a live chicken! Dey don't allow no live animals on de bus."
>
> The old woman considered a moment. "All right, boss." She stepped to one side and she wrung the chicken's neck.

Reading Rhyne's books brought back to me vivid memories of my grandmother. When we, as Rhyne did, record the history around us as stories, we create precious legacies for generations to come.

We must work to save the tales that reflect our cultural diversity. Scientists tell us that ecological diversity may hold important keys to problems we encounter today. Similarly, returning to our cultural roots by revisiting stories told by our ancestors may also unlock the answers to our modern problems.

DISTINCTIONS BETWEEN CLASSICAL STORYTELLING AND TELLING STORIES FROM THE PLATFORM

Today's professional speakers are creating a new body of work, which could be considered as a new branch of the classical storytelling tree. However, significant differences exist between the world of the classical storyteller and that of the professional speaker.

1. **Purpose of the story.** When a professional speaker tells a story, the story expands or explains a key point in the presentation. The majority of the time, the speaker will tell the story and reiterate the point the story makes. When a storyteller tells a story, the story is the presentation and the point is left for the listener to discern, unless the story is a parable or moral tale.

2. **Setting.** Professional speakers typically present in business or professional settings. Conference centers, meeting rooms, auditoriums, and training rooms are the usual locations for a presentation by a professional speaker. Storytellers often present in schools, libraries, and special settings such as parks or bookstores.

3. **Audience.** By and large, professional speakers address adults or young adults. Storytellers traditionally addressed audiences of children but today have diversified so that they also appeal to adults.

4. **Numbers of stories told.** A professional speaker may use 5 to 15 stories in an hour-long presentation. A classical storyteller will probably tell only 1 to 3 stories per hour.

5. **Length of the story.** A story told by a professional speaker may take less than three minutes to tell because

each story is but a part of a presentation. Storytellers will spin out a yarn because it is the presentation itself.

6. **Characters in the story.** A story told by a professional speaker will be about people, often businesspeople, sometimes friends, family, or acquaintances. A storyteller may tell an entire tale populated by animals or superhuman beings such as fairies.

   "The elements or characters may not be as common or as readily identifiable in classical storytelling tradition, because the storyteller's job is to encourage the audience's imagination," explains Sharon Jones, director of membership, National Storytelling Association.

7. **Origin of the story.** The finest professional speakers on the platform today create, craft, and present their own personal stories. Storytellers draw from an existing body of story literature, which relies heavily on traditional stories handed down orally from generation to generation.

8. **Ownership of the story.** Ethical professional speakers are limited to telling either stories they have created or paraphrasing stories they have read. Rarely will professional speakers use another's story, even with permission, because when a meeting planner engages a professional speaker, that meeting planner expects fresh or unique material. Storytellers may decide to share a story they have created themselves, to draw from an existing body of work, or to tell a story created by another storyteller with permission. For classical storytellers, drawing from an established body of work is both acceptable and desirable. In their book *Storytelling: Process & Practice,* Norma J. Livo and Sandra A. Rietz note, "A storyteller is a living library . . . the repository of literature."

Storytellers are charged by Livo and Rietz with the responsibility of passing on information and training other storytellers: "Therefore, many cultures have devised elaborate techniques for choosing and training storytellers to keep the stories from being extinguished—techniques involving a redundancy of storytellers and a redundancy of information."

On the opposite end of the spectrum lies professional speaking. Speakers delight in teaching each other about presenting, collecting stories, and developing stories, but—and this is a huge "but"—stories created by the speaker are **proprietary and remain forever the property of the creator.** The only exception to this occurs when one speaker agrees with another to share material.

THEFT AND PROFESSIONAL SPEAKING

Following the publication of Mark Victor Hansen's and Jack Canfield's book *Chicken Soup for the Soul,* professional speakers were awash in calls to write stories for inclusion in similar anthologies. Many speakers responded happily, buoyed by the Hansen and Canfield bestseller. Other speakers refused to participate, saying; "If my stories are published, will that make it easier for other speakers to take them?" This is a valid concern because many nonprofessional and beginning speakers take material verbatim from books or articles they've read and neglect to credit the sources. Certainly, if you wish to become an expert, you must do research. But research becomes theft when you take other people's material and pass it off as your own. When a novice speaker hears another speaker's story and decides to "borrow" that material, an act of theft has been committed. Seems harmless enough, doesn't it? It's not. That story is as proprietary as a painting, a song, or any other work of art. The original speaker may have worked for months to perfect that story. Using another speaker's material is theft, pure and simple, and it is no different from stealing a can of cola from a grocery store.

There is no good reason to steal material. Within you lies a world of stories and materials that is uniquely yours. After reading this book and working through the materials presented here, you will be able to create your own material.

TIP   Chicken Soup for the Soul, Chicken Soup for the Soul at Work, Where the Heart Is . . . Stories of Home & Family, *and* Chocolate for a Woman's Soul *are filled with examples of the types of stories that professional speakers use. Buy yourself all these books. Read them carefully and note which stories appeal most to you. We all have a storytelling personality. What I tell may not work for you—emotionally or content wise. By using these fine anthologies as guides, you'll develop an idea of what types of stories fit you.*

Theft of their best stuff is an all-too-common reality for platform professionals. In this book, unless otherwise noted, you will be reading stories from my personal inventory. If you repeat these stories as your own, you will cheat yourself, your audiences, and your career. The time you spend memorizing these stories detracts from time you could have spent developing your own, unique materials.

SUMMARY

Stories vary by their length, type of characters, deeds, and purpose. *Classical storytelling* refers to an art that sprang from dramatic narratives and typically uses stylized tales that have often come from folklore. Classical storytelling and telling stories from the platform differ in significant ways by audience, setting, purpose, number of stories told, length of story, characters, origin of the story, and ownership of the story.

EXERCISES

1. What were your favorite stories as a child? Write down as much as you can remember about your favorite story. Review a book of fairy tales by the Grimm brothers or by Hans Christian Andersen. Compare how you remember the story with the version in the book.

2. Explore books of fairy tales and folklore from other cultures. What similarities exist between these stories and the stories you heard growing up?

3. Go to see a professional storyteller. Take notes. Divide your page into two halves: The Story and The Delivery. Note how the words and the delivery work together to tell the story. Observe how involved the audience is or isn't.

4. Choose a fairy tale to tell to a group. Make the characters as different from each other as you can by using your voice. Consider what gestures might enhance the story.

5. Find an example of each of the types of stories listed. Identify the sequence of action, the complicating situation, the sympathetic character, and the solution.

4 Where Stories Come From

I am really moved by your story . . . All my friends never heard a story like this, I am sure—if I invite you to my home, would you tell this story to all my friends?

> Vladimir Horowitz asking piano tuner Franz Mohr to tell the story of his spiritual awakening, quoted in *My Life with the Great Pianists* by Franz Mohr

Telling a story is more than entertainment. It's a form of conversation, and also a way of remembering a certain kind of rhythm.

> Lewis Nordan, quoted in *Writing for Your Life #2,* edited by Sybil Steinberg

Women must turn to one another for stories; they must share the stories of their lives and their hopes and their unacceptable fantasies.

> Carolyn G. Heilbrun, *Writing a Woman's Life*

WHO YOU ARE . . .

You are a walking universe of stories. You are the story of your parents' meeting, of the wild ride to the hospital the night your mother first felt contractions, and of how your parents chose your name.

Each cell within you carries the stamp of who you are and how you live and what you have eaten. Dagwood, the comic-strip character, often sits with his children and talks about photos in the family album. Spend time with your family album, and get back in touch with who you are and your personal history. Turn inside and draw on the incredible wealth of your own life experience.

FINDING STORIES

Picture a shimmering summer day on the river. You rent a canoe and decide to take a float trip and go fishing. You have three choices about how to get bait: (1) You can use a seine, a net that scoops the silver shivering minnows into your bucket. (2) You can borrow bait from another boater. (3) You can buy bait from a store.

You'll use three similar techniques to find stories: (1) You can use your net to catch the stories that travel in the stream of your life, current and past. (2) You can interview people about their lives or research stories and use these stories *with permission*. (3) You can buy books and tapes and relate stories you hear. (The best source for this is a biography, from which you can borrow stories, credit the source, and not be stealing.)

Finding the Stories in Your Life

A journalism teacher gave his class an assignment: Write a story about an exciting experience that happened to you personally.

A few hours after class, a sophomore knocked on the teacher's door. She explained that she had a problem with the assignment because nothing exciting had ever happened to her.

"Do you mean that you've never met anyone exciting? Done anything exciting? Seen anything exciting? And you've never been anywhere exciting?" probed the teacher. "Well, have you ever been on vacation?"

Yes, she had traveled with her family to the Grand Canyon.

"What was that like? In rugged country like that, a lot can happen. Were you hiking?"

Yes, but only part of the way.

"Why?"

The student blushed. "I got bitten by a rattlesnake and lost consciousness," she said. "My family had to go get help. Finally, the EMTs came and lifted me out in a sling tied to an emergency helicopter."

The point? Some people wouldn't know a good story if it bit them. (Pun intended.) Or as Frank P. Thomas writes in *How to Write the Story of Your Life,* "There are golden nuggets of personal history waiting to be mined out of every life."

Some Folks Got It and So Do You

Occasionally, a person in my audience will ask, "Do all those crazy things really happen to you? If they do, you must live a really weird life because nothing like that ever happens to me."

Of course weird things happen to you. But, unlike a trained storyteller, you neglect to notice those weird things. Your life is full of stories waiting to be told. "People can be viewed in some sense as repositories of stories," explains Roger C. Schank. And finding them isn't a matter of luck. Jon Franklin points out that if the stories he discovered—and later won a Pulitzer Prize for—were simply the result of luck, he'd "lose his nerve and, as a result, his livelihood."

To find the stories in your life, you must be what humorist Jeanne Robertson calls a "trained noticer." Robertson should know; she has built a career on the kind of humor that springs from "the believable, daily mingling of human beings." In *How to Be Funny,* Steve Allen says, "Unless there are comic poltergeists at work, however, there is no apparent reason why a Woody Allen should have more amusing experiences than a Ronald Reagan. The comedian's experiences are probably no more amusing than others'; he or she simply has a certain sensitivity to the environment and circumstances and so perceives humor that a more serious person might miss."

How can you learn to be a trained noticer? That person with a "certain sensitivity to the environment and circumstances"? You must

1. believe that the stories and humorous situations are out there;
2. learn to see with a storyteller's eye; and
3. be willing to let stories develop—like bread, they need time to rise, fall, and rise again before they become delicious. Professional speakers often work on a story for years, searching to find the perfect order of telling, the right words, and the well-timed pause. We'll discuss how to work on your stories in Chapter 6.

Let's face it. Unless you are an Olympic athlete, a politician, a movie star, or some other type of celebrity, you need something to talk about if you are going to be a speaker. The best source of material is your life. Grady Jim Robinson says, "There must be millions of stories inside each individual." The challenge is retrieving and shaping them.

Believe the Stories Are Out There

Of course, if you don't believe that there are stories in your life ripe for the picking, you won't ever see them. You have unconsciously affirmed that your life has nothing to offer.

Affirmations retrain our thinking. Habitual thoughts represent the mental equivalent of ruts in a gravel road. The more times you drive in the rut, the deeper it becomes, and the harder it is to get back out.

Ever since you were little, you were told that before you cross the street, you have to look left and then look right. You've probably heard this millions of times, and you've probably repeated it to yourself countless times as well, and now it is a habit.

One day, however, you are walking out of a hotel in London, and the bellhop reminds you, "Don't forget! You Yanks drive on the wrong side of the road. Here you must look right and then left or you'll get smashed flat in the street. Too right!"

For the first few street crossings, you do as you are told. Then, you start to cross a street and what do you do? You look *left and then right!* Why? Because you have affirmed "look left and then right" so often that you followed those directions unconsciously. Similarly, if you affirm "nothing worth talking about ever happens to me," you'll unconsciously believe that, too. As a result, you may reject stories or story seedlings which could have turned into beautiful, strong oak trees with a little loving care.

THE REAL MEANING OF STORIES

John was learning the content of a program necessary to become a trainer, and he was frustrated. He had listened to one trainer after another present materials. Each seasoned trainer drew from a bounteous supply of stories, examples, and quotations.

"I'll never have the stories you guys do!" he said in exasperation.

And he's right. He'll never have the same stories the other trainers have, but someday he'll have stories of his own. When you begin your career as speaker or trainer, the task of finding stories can seem daunting. Unless you are a natural raconteur, both remembering and telling stories can seem hard. John was convinced he had no stories to draw from, and yet, that very morning, he had shared a super story about having to inch his way around a second-story, 12-inch ledge toward an open window in his apartment because he had locked himself out and his training materials inside. As John hung precariously onto the building, his next-door neighbor peered out her bathroom window and yelled to her husband, "Come quick! There's a guy in a suit, tie, and wingtips trying to break into the apartment building next door!" When John was reminded of his story, he said, "But what does that have to do with business?"

As of that moment, John's story had no point and no theme. Nor do most stories in the beginning. That's why we must work with them. Don't get discouraged if you have a great story that doesn't seem to make a point. Eventually you will find a way to use the story.

Here are three tips for the beginning storyteller:

1. **Don't judge your stories in the beginning.** If John decides that that story about the ledge is useless, he will forget the anecdote and never have the chance to see it develop. Homeless today is not necessarily homeless tomorrow. Don't be too rough on your stories.
2. **Don't compare your stories with those of others.** People who have been speaking for years have collected a lot of material. That's part of the job. You'll have a truckload of stories in 20 years, too, if you work at it. Remember: Experts estimate that becoming a good speaker doesn't happen for most people until they've been speaking for 10 years. Be patient.

3. **Don't worry about how to use your stories in the beginning.** This can become a vicious circle. You can't see how to use the story so you forget it. Because you have no raw material to work with, you never experience developing a story. Because you never develop a story, you never try to put a moral with it. And so it goes.

STORY-FINDING AFFIRMATIONS

Use these affirmations to awaken your subconscious mind. By asking your subconscious to help you in your quest for stories, you are enlisting a powerful ally. "The unlimited power of the subconscious mind resembles the vastness of the heavens," says Joyce Chapman in her book *Journaling for Joy.*

Be sure to repeat each of these affirmations three times on a daily basis for at least two weeks, making sure your final repetition reflects total conviction.

1. My life is a rich and abundant source of great stories.
2. As I review my past, I find many terrific ideas and stories to use in my speaking.
3. Great stories come to me daily.

To further assist you in your search for material, write the word *stories* on three index cards and post them in prominent places.

MINING YOUR LIFE

Who are you? What have you done? Where are you going? You are like an iceberg. We look at you and see you as you exist in present time and space. All that you have experienced remains hidden, but still a part of you. When you speak, you share with me a look at the submerged part of the iceberg, the you that remains hidden from the outside world but essential to who you are.

When we are willing to share, we literally invite our listeners into our lives. The gap between the lectern and the audience narrows, and we both experience greater satisfaction with our interaction. The Johari Window (see Figure 4.1) offers us another way to explore this idea.

The Johari Window

Arena

The ARENA represents that which we know about ourselves that we gladly share with others. This would be our past, our habits, our preferences, and so on. This area offers a

Figure 4.1

THE JOHARI WINDOW

I know You know **ARENA**	I don't know You know **BLIND SPOT**
FACADE I know You don't know	**POTENTIAL** I don't know You don't know

Adapted from *Group Processes: An Introduction to Group Dynamics,* Third Edition by Joseph Luft. Copyright © 1984, 1970, 1963 by Joseph Luft. Reprinted by permission of Mayfield Publishing Company.

rich mother lode of stories as we mine our past for incidents we can share from the platform.

Blind Spot

The BLIND SPOT represents that which other people know of us but that we can't see about ourselves. Ed, a speaker, critiques a tape made by another speaker, Nancy. Ed tells her, "Do you know you must have used the word *lovely* about 56 times?" He continues, "That's definitely a woman's word! The first few times I could handle it, but about halfway through the tape, I thought I'd go bonkers." Nancy appreciates the critique because her BLIND SPOT did not allow her to hear her overuse of a word. Can you retrieve stories from this window? The BLIND SPOT only becomes available to you if you are open to new information.

Facade

The FACADE window represents that which we know and don't wish to share. Here we find painful instances that could become stories in time or with perspective. We also turn to this arena to find those stories that we would share only under the right circumstances. For example, Rosita Perez assesses her audience and then decides how much to share with them about the impact of multiple sclerosis (MS) on her life. For one audience, she might refrain from sharing the indignities the illness has caused. With nurses, a frank discussion of how MS has changed her life might be wholly appropriate. This window must be examined periodically and considered with care. What was once difficult for us to share may now be not only appropriate but also perfect.

Potential

The POTENTIAL window represents the unknown and operates only in the present or the future. When we share the stories of our lives with a live audience and experience its feedback, we tap that unknown potential. The unknown potential represents that which we cannot predict and cannot control. One speaker told of his life as the son of Holocaust survivors. Obviously, that was information from his past, his known and available window. After he spoke, a line of people waited to speak to him. Most of the people related his comments back to their own lives—even though they were not the children of Holocaust survivors! They heard his story and compared it to similar situations they had encountered. The new stories they shared with him represented new ideas that might not have been tapped had he not shared himself first. Together, the speaker and the listeners created another new story, the one you are reading now.

When speakers share, the audience feels compelled to do the same, and we witness a phenomenon called disclosure matching, a conversational quid pro quo. In *The Talk Book: The Intimate Science of Communicating in Close Relationships,* Gerald Goodman explains the value of this transaction: "No disclosures, no intimacy. Without disclosure matching we would all live in perpetual isolation."

The best speakers share of themselves in a manner that is so universal, so true that we see ourselves in their stories— despite the differences in our experiences. While speaking, we invite disclosure matching when we share a personal anecdote with our audiences. Whether or not audience members stay after to talk with you, you can be sure your personal anecdotes set off a dialogue of give and take in your listeners' minds. Your authentic life will always interest your audience because your sharing allows them to process their own lives as well.

Ways to Mine Your Life

Remember the old prospector who seemed to appear in every Western? He'd wave his pick and his pan over his head and holler, "There's gold in them thar hills!" Yep, there surely is. Be aware, however, that to get to the gold you need to dig through a lot of dirt, slosh through a river's worth of water, and toss a lot of fool's gold. But when you come upon that perfect, pure nugget, you'll be rewarded.

Remember, too, that the old prospector rarely pulled goose-egg-sized lumps out of the ground. You won't either. As you travel through this chapter, look for story nuggets, small bits of thought that could be coaxed into growing into big, beautiful gold chunks. How will you recognize a story nugget? Look for ideas that strike you as worth exploring, for emotions that strike resonant chords, and for characters you'd like to get to know better.

CAUTION: MEMORY LOSS CAN BE A PROTECTIVE MEASURE

Jim has no memories at all of his early life. No matter what you ask him, or how you encourage him, Jim comes up blank.

A few of us can't remember because the minutiae of today have crowded yesterday out of our minds. A few of us can't remember because our memories are too painful. Therapists report that when people have had horrific childhoods, they often suppress their memories until their own children reach the age they were when the memory happened. In other words, if your mother was diagnosed as having cancer when you were eight, you might suppress that memory until your own child becomes eight. At that time, because of your involvement with your child, your old memories may surface.

Therefore, if any of these exercises become uncomfortable, put them aside. If these exercises arouse intense emotions, you might want to talk to a trained counselor about what you are feeling. Under no circumstances should you continue if you are feeling overwhelmingly depressed, angry, or sad. On the other hand, if your mining brings up emotions you can handle, great. As Grady Jim Robinson says, "You're getting to the real stuff." You've probably hit on a valuable story for yourself and your listeners. When and when not to share a story will be covered in Chapter 7.

MINING FOR GOLD FROM YOUR PAST

Miners knew what land formations were most likely to indicate a rich vein of gold was right below the surface. Here are land formations you can prospect to find the gold in your life.

1. Examine Your Journal

If you've kept a journal, congratulations. You probably have all the story ideas you can handle. If not, now might be a good time to start.

The methods of journal writers are highly individualistic. One speaker keeps notes on each page of her day-timer. Another uses her computer to keep a diary, reasoning that she can keyboard faster than she can write. A journalist may record the happenings of the world around him. Another may only jot down interesting happenings on an irregular basis. Speaker, author, and inspirational guru Tony Robbins often mentions his journals, pointing out that if your life is worth living, it is worth recording.

Beyond providing you with a tangible record of daily events which may preserve stories and story seedlings for you, the act of journaling will help you organize your world—past and present—mentally. In *Writing Yourself Home: A Woman's Guided Journey of Self Discovery,* Kimberley Snow provides a wonderful, structured approach to journaling. Snow points out that "writing releases us into a timeless world where all things are possible. . . . Through writing and visualization we are able to develop a personal language that fills out the hollows and blank spaces in our lives, to make sense of and give reality to our experience." Whether you are male or female, Snow's exercises titled "Writing for Pleasure" will help you generate stories from your innermost self.

Another version of journaling can be found in *The Artist's Way,* in which Julia Cameron lists "morning pages" as one of the pivotal tools in creative recovery. She defines them as "three pages of longhand writing stream-of-consciousness." Cameron suggests that these pages capture "all the whiny petty stuff that . . . stands between you and your creativity."

Perhaps you have begun to wonder, "Why so much writing if what I want to do is to speak?" Writing begets discovery. William Zinsser says in *Writing to Learn,* "It's by writing about a subject we're trying to learn that we reason our way to what it means." He goes on to explain,

> Writing organizes and clarifies our thoughts. Writing is
> how we think our way into a subject and make it our
> own. Writing enables us to find out what we know—and
> what we don't know—about whatever we're trying to
> learn. . . . Whatever we write—a memo, a letter, a note to
> the baby-sitter—all of us know this moment of finding out
> what we really want to say by trying in writing to say it.

For the speaker, no single exercise can be more valuable than writing. Speaking by its nature is ethereal. We speak and the words are gone. But by reexamining them on paper, we save, refine, and define our message. Writing keeps us from falling off the keen edge of speaking into the abyss of chattering.

Your journal need not be a finely written document in order to serve you. But using your journal as a catch-all for your life experiences gives you a quick and immediate first draft for your future rewrites.

2. Review Your Photograph Album

Using a notebook, jot down a couple of words about each photo. Sit down with your family, especially your parents or grandparents and siblings. What do they remember about each photo?

As you look at each photo, examine the surroundings carefully. What can you see in each picture? Your home? Your school? A pet or favorite toy? Make notes on what you remember about each location.

Actor and speech coach Max Dixon suggests drawing a floor plan of a place you lived in before the age of 12. Be as complete as possible. Put in the gas fake fireplace. Make a note about the color of the wallpaper. Label your bedroom. The next step, according to Dixon, involves mapping out your emotional responses. Where did you feel safe? Which room held happy memories? Reconstructing your physical environment helps you get back in touch with the child you were. As Robinson says, "You can't get away from your childhood. It's always there." Childhood stories work well with audiences of all demographics because we were all children once.

3. Interview a Person from Your Past

Ask teachers, relatives, or friends what they remember about you growing up. Bonus idea: Bring along a list of historic events that happened during their lives and ask what they were doing at the time. You'll also glean stories of their lives and the people they have known.

The Timetables of History, by Bernard Grun, ranks as my favorite resource for reviewing the past. Grun has divided each historical time period into seven sections: history and politics; literature and theater; religion, philosophy, and learning; visual arts; music; science, technology, and growth; and daily life. By mentioning happenings in each of these columns, you can ignite all kinds of memories. Looking at the book for the year 1958 might remind you that you were in kindergarten when the American flag changed as we added Alaska as a state.

Of course, you will also want to ask others what they remember about you. One woman who had grown up in an abusive environment interviewed her aunt. She was astonished to hear the aunt say, "When you were little, I was so upset about the way your father treated you that I went to my husband with my concerns. But . . . my husband told me to keep out of it. He said that what your daddy did was his business—and he reminded me that your father would probably turn his terrible temper on me if I persisted." This small story gave the interviewer an entirely new perspective on her childhood: "Before I talked to my aunt, my impression was that perhaps I had deserved my father's mistreatment and anger. After this conversation, I realized I was innocent, and I realized that even the adults around me cowered before my father." As a result, the interviewer was able to rethink her childhood and pick up stories that she otherwise might have avoided.

Use a tape recorder for the sessions and you'll also preserve voices and dialects which may help you when you actually prepare your stories for presentation.

4. Research Your Family Tree

Using a book such as *Tracing Your Ancestry Logbook,* by F. Wilbur Helmbold, you can even discover the tales told by your dead ancestors. For example, one woman with striking red hair and pale skin found out her relatives were Cherokees. Bonus idea: Not only did she learn more about herself, but she also has a lead on an interesting story about a pair of star-crossed lovers who built a nest in her family tree.

5. Dust Off Your High School Yearbook

The most fascinating characters we meet in stories are those people who change and grow. While a few of us don't change a bit after graduating from high school, thankfully, others of us move on. The movie *Peggie Sue Got Married* revolves around a woman's flashback to her life in high school. If your high school career was a movie, how would it look? Cast the principal players. Note the concerns and dramas you responded to. Bonus idea: As you search for yourself in your yearbook, you'll also pick up great stories about other people. Consider each person in each picture as a book you've read halfway through. How does the book end? What has become of the people you walked the halls with?

You may even want to attend a high school reunion with an undercover reporter mindset. Sheldon attended his reunion and was shocked to hear that his old girlfriend had broken up with the high school football star she married. The reason: Mr. Football had punched out his wife's front teeth in a drunken rage. The former athlete straggled into the reunion and sat on the edge of the action the entire weekend. Intrigued, Sheldon went over and spoke to Mr. Football. Sheldon learned that 20 years later, the high school's star athlete was now an unemployed drifter. "And to think," said Sheldon, "I once thought I wanted to be like him." For a few of us, high school represents the apex of our lives; by attending a reunion, Sheldon came back with a powerful story about role modeling.

Michael Scott Karpovich uses his high school experience to great advantage in his presentations. A self-described nerd, "Karp" was regularly victimized by a group of bullies. The inspirational story of how he learned to take care of his life has given him a unique platform presence.

6. Go Back Physically (or Mentally) to a Place from Your Past

One morning as I was walking, a whiff of the dew-covered pine trees transported me mentally to my grandmother's house in South Carolina. On the walls of her parlor were the portraits painted of my ancestors. In gloomy, dark colors, two men and a woman stared down at me from their worlds bordered by gilt plaster frames. What I learned as a child was that I was part of a long line of people. I do not stand alone in history. The end of the thread is mine to carry forward into the next generation. This gave me a powerful sense of purpose.

What you see or smell or taste can evoke powerful memories. Go back through your mother's recipe box, buy a candy you loved as a child, and walk through a toy store and check out a Hula Hoop or a Slinky.

Paying attention to the world all around you can yield marvelous story ideas, which in turn can be the focal points for an entire program. Mari Pat Varga had forgotten the phrase "popcorn player" until an article in *Time* magazine quoted Kevin McHale talking about a new NBA player as a "popcorn player." Memories of Varga's career as a high school basketball player came flooding back, and she was in touch with the idea of "a player who explodes into full size when he or she enters the stadium, hears the roar of the crowd, sees the brilliant lights, feels the leather surface of the basketball, and smells the popcorn." Varga remembered a popcorn player as one "who is prepared for the peak performance, pulls it off, and exceeds all expectations." With this new insight, Varga was able to create stories and a program called "Popcorn Player Performance: How to Turn On the Heat When the Pressure Is On." She describes the program as "how to prepare to perform at peak levels when we face our biggest challenges—the opposing team, an angry customer, co-workers, or our own attitudes."

TIP *Share your favorite experience with a friend. What recipes remind him or her of home? What favorite toy does your friend remember? What candy couldn't your pal get enough of then—and today? By sparking ideas off another person, you may rekindle the smoldering embers of an old memory.*

7. Try a Synergy Exercise

Synergy is defined by the *American New Heritage Dictionary* as "the action of two or more substances . . . to achieve an effect of which each is individually incapable." Natalie Goldberg explains synergy in *Writing Down the Bones* as "1 + 1 = Mercedes Benz." Synergy is creative energy in action.

The following exercise will help you put synergy to work finding your life stories. Copy the following lists of words onto sheets of colored paper so that each list is on a different color.

mother	Halloween	belts	delight
father	Christmas	fish	angry
sister	Easter	water	scared
brother	Passover	basket	surprise
grandmother	July 4th	furniture	comfort
grandfather	Memorial Day	turkey	laugh
minister	spring	cookies	teach
neighbor	fall	hospital	pour
movie star	winter	kitchen	dissolve
friend	summer	bicycle	jump
adult	vacation	clock	splash
boss	Monday	desk	hop
pet	weekend	car	trip
teacher	Friday	notebook	contrast
choir	Sunday	book	sing
pilot	evening	hot-air balloon	float
doctor	morning	medicine	gulp
enemy	lunch	dog	sneak
camp counselor	birthday	present	return

Now, cut the paper apart so that you have only single words on little slips of paper. Shuffle all the words in each pile. Taking one word of each color, tickle your memory.

This list may assist you in remembering all sorts of experiences: a car drive with a vomiting dog, a band camp where you marched at dawn to the top of a mountain in Tennessee, and a neighbor who had a hot-air balloon.

You can extend this list easily. One way is to choose a category and make another list. You can also simply pick random words from the newspaper or from the yellow pages. The more disparate the items are on your lists, the better chances you'll have of jogging your memory.

8. Relive Your Holidays, Ceremonies, Rituals, and Traditions

Certain times of year and rituals of our lives loom large in our memories. A toastmaster at a wedding raised a glass of champagne and noted, "As I watched this bride and groom make their wedding vows, my thoughts returned with love to my own marriage and the joy I take in my relationship with my wife." So we all return to those special moments that remain ever clear in our minds. What holidays, ceremonies, rituals, or traditions do you recall?

A Christian church decided to hold a seder ceremony to familiarize its members with what Jesus actually celebrated during the Last Supper. The minister invited his friend David, a Jew, to lead the seder. Although he followed the traditional service, the Haggadah, David also shared stories of the Passovers he had celebrated as a child. "Traditionally, at this point in the service, an outside door must be opened to admit the spirit of Elijah," explained David. "But one year, after my mother opened the door, we heard a sharp rap. My bewildered mom answered the door and found an FBI agent on our threshold. My mom had been a schoolteacher, and the agent was doing a background check on one of her former students. I was only eight, but my brother and I were so amazed by this odd turn of events that every year thereafter, we'd announce during the seder, 'Here's Elijah from the FBI.'"

David's personal memory added greatly to the seder service. Not only did he share the traditional ceremony but also David enriched the service by seasoning the evening with his memories of growing up Jewish. For months afterward, church members talked about the service. Your memories of special times are rich, wide veins of gold.

TIP *One of the best books for exploring personal stories is also the smallest.* Telling Your Own Stories, *by Donald Davis, fits neatly in your purse or backpack. Davis relies on "prompts," which he likens to "the metaphor of a baited fishhook." By going through his "prompts" with your family, you glean a two-fer activity: material for stories and wholesome entertainment.*

9. Review Your Roles

To explore all aspects of yourself, Max Dixon suggests quickly making a list of words that describe you. Here are a few terms to get you started:

student	bike rider	churchgoer
friend	speaker	sibling
questioner	listener	car owner

According to Dixon, stories have three important ingredients: conflict, decision, and discovery. Using those three words, compare each of them to your list of roles. Can you think of a time when you had to make a decision as a car owner?

One presenter generated this:

I remember my favorite car, a fire-engine red 450 SL Mercedes Benz convertible. I had had a great time driving with the top down around the campus where I taught. I'd pull up to a stoplight and peer over the top of my sunglasses to see handsome college hunks staring at me. The best part, though, was watching the expression change on their faces when I got out of the car—and the hunksters realized I was nine months pregnant! With a baby on the way, and the car always needing repairs, I came to a tough decision: I sold it. I'll never forget rocking my newborn son in my arms and hearing the man who bought it kick the tires one more time before my husband handed him the keys.

KEEPING YOUR PRESENTATION BALANCED

Your audience will reject you if you are the focal point of all your stories. A talented speaker once made a fool of himself during a presentation to other speakers when he told one story after another in which he was the hero. He rescued this Fortune 500 company and that one and helped the CEO of this major industry and that . . . and who cares? As he ran out the door (he was far too busy to stick around and chat, of course), the entire room breathed a sigh of relief. The evaluations ranked him very low. The message is clear: You can't be the hero of all your stories.

Hogging the limelight tells the audience more about your ego than about life in general. Furthermore, when you hog the limelight, your presentation lacks variety. Instead, you need to maintain what Patricia Fripp calls the "I–You Ratio." John Cantu, a comedy-writing coach, showed Fripp the importance of this technique for bringing the audience into the story, as Fripp explains in an article originally published in *Professional Speaker* magazine.

> For example, if a female comedian says, "Well, I was a cheerleader when . . . " before she gets to the punch line, most people in the audience are thinking, "She

must think she's something special," or, "My thighs were too fat to be a cheerleader."

However, if she says, "Have you ever had an experience so embarrassing that you wanted the ground to open up and swallow you?" the audience members start nodding their heads. "Let me tell you about when I was a cheerleader."

In this approach, a statement directs the audience members to look into themselves—and instantly, the rapport builds.

Whenever possible, the speaker strives to pull the audience into the presentation. By being aware of the "I–You Ratio," we can do this effectively. As Michael M. Klepper says in *I'd Rather Die Than Give a Speech*, "The key word here is balance, a mixture of what you see and say, what people on the scene have witnessed, and what others can favorably attest to when it comes to the work you're doing."

INTERVIEWING OTHER PEOPLE

One way to spread the glory of the spotlight is by interviewing other people. You can uncover wonderful anecdotes to add to your inventory of stories. Interviewing others represents an important way to broaden your story repertoire for a variety of reasons.

1. By Interviewing, You Can Add the Stories of People of Different Backgrounds

If you are not 80 years old, if you haven't worked in a manufacturing facility, and if you've never been a member of a minority group, you might have difficulty relating to audiences of octogenarians, blue-collar workers, and Hispanics. But, by interviewing people from different walks of life, you can know and share a variety of viewpoints by telling the stories of an 80-year-old, a plant worker, and a minority-group member.

Your interviewing process does not have to be formal. Instead, take advantage of the opportunities presented in your daily life to ask people, "What is life like for you?"

By asking and listening purposefully, you will hear remarkable tales. An 80-year-old woman told a speaker, "I love life. I can't wait to get up every day and see what happens!" Since she was a retired member of the organization the speaker was addressing, the presenter was delighted to share her sentiments from the platform. By honoring her and her philosophy of life, the speaker honored the entire group.

2. By Interviewing Others, You Can Share Stories Pertinent to Your Audience's Industry or Occupation

When I interviewed my mother about her work in food service, I was able to share her insights later in my presentation to that industry. By interviewing anyone you know in the industry you're presenting to, you will uncover a wealth of information, attitudes, and insider's insights.

I asked my mother, "What's the most important idea you've taken away from your work in food preparation?" She thought a moment and then replied, "I've learned there are no mistakes. If you burn the meat, you trim off the burned area, cut it into chunks, cover it with gravy and serve it over rice as chow mein. If your gelatin doesn't set, you add fruit cocktail and put whipped cream on top to make it a fruit parfait. Nothing is ever wasted." Sharing this philosophy from the platform helped me to bond with the audience. They appreciated the fact that I had taken the time to get to know their industry and its problems. People don't expect you to know every word of jargon or every nuance of what they do. However, when you take the time to explore their world, you validate the way they've chosen to spend their lives.

One speaker called an industry expert and asked for a phone appointment. "I simply explained that everyone told me he was the person they looked up to in their industry, and I asked if I could have 15 minutes of his time on my dime. The gentleman consented. My homework really paid off with my audience."

By interviewing key people in your audience's industry, you can share pertinent stories that meet the audience's needs and expectations.

TIP *You can improve your interviewing skills by watching television talk-show hosts. Note how they use open-ended and close-ended questions. An open-ended question generates the most information because it is a question that cannot be answered with a one-word answer. A close-ended question helps you focus and offers a great way to double-check the facts.*

Open-Ended Questions

What is it you enjoy about your work?

How do you do what you do?

What is the funniest thing that has ever happened to you at work?

What regrets do you have?

Close-Ended Questions

How many years have you worked here?

Do you like what you do?

Can I repeat your story in a presentation?

3. Ask Other Speakers If They Have Stories That They Are Willing To Let You Use

Once in a while, a speaker may stumble across a story that another speaker may be willing to share.

For example, Michael Brandwein had an interesting experience with an audience of recreation and park professionals who were taking copious notes during his presentation. In contrast, three gentlemen sat motionless with arms folded across their chests, not taking a single note. During the lunch break, Brandwein happened to return prematurely to the seminar room and found the men surreptitiously copying notes he had made on the flip chart. Brandwein realized that these men were probably concerned about saving face during his presentation. Brandwein uses this story, and he also gave another speaker permission to use the story, because it fit into the speaker's area of expertise, gender communications.

HOW TO CONDUCT A
GREAT INTERVIEW

In preparation for your presentation, ask the meeting planner to give you the names and numbers of at least five people who will be attending your session. Put on your interviewer's hat and use this time to dig for stories. Of course, most people won't be able to share a story with you off the cuff, but you can prompt them by getting them into the right frame of mind. Start by preparing an introduction for your call:

> Hi, I'm Jane Doe, and I'm presenting a workshop for your association next month. If you have a few minutes, I'd like to ask for your feedback. Your comments are important because I'll use them to help me tailor a presentation that really meets the needs of your group. Can you help me?

Then put together a few questions:

- When you can't sleep at night because you're thinking about your job, what are you thinking?

- ▪ Tell me something funny that has happened to you in your work. Anything that happened that you and your co-workers still laugh about?
- ▪ Tell me what you like best and least about your work.
- ▪ What is the biggest misconception about your work?
- ▪ What's the weirdest situation that's happened at work?
- ▪ Tell me something interesting about your work.

Carole Hyatt, author of *The Woman's New Selling Game: How to Sell Yourself and Anything Else,* says that while interviewing people for her books, she would encourage them to talk by saying, "Tell me more . . . uuummm . . . interesting . . . (and then repeating their last words)." With this prodding, they would talk on and on, revealing themselves to her. Hyatt would not speak except to prompt more information. To her surprise, her subject would remark, "Carole, YOU are the most fascinating person I've ever met." As Dewitt Jones, speaker and *National Geographic* photographer, says, "There are stories all around us."

Being a good listener is hard work, but if you watch Oprah Winfrey, you'll see an expert extract the best from her guests. Take a few cues from Oprah:

1. Reflect the person's comments back to them. "So you stood there while the boss had a temper tantrum . . . "
2. Empathize or react to the emotion. "And you must have felt embarrassed knowing his fly was unzipped . . . "
3. Encourage the person to go on. "What happened next?"

Occasionally you will phone a person who can't help you. Ask the person to recommend whom you should call. Every group has a "live wire," an eager contributor of information.

GETTING YOUR SUBJECTS TO TALK

People become guarded and formal when they think their comments are being carefully recorded. Don't be disappointed if the phone call generates minimal results. Journalists often find that the best quotations come after the notebook is closed and the pen is put away. Relaxed people tell the best stories, but getting people to feel relaxed takes effort.

In my years as a television talk show host, I noticed that my guests would freeze up the moment the camera person indicated we were on the air. Once we hosted the incoming president of the local real estate association, a gentleman who was clearly impressed with himself. He sprawled in his chair and tossed back his sun-streaked hair while he adjusted his sunglasses. (Unusual, since we were in the middle of a soybean field in Illinois, not a beach in California.) He studied his manicure and flicked his hair back from his eyes as we waited to go "On Air." Then the camera person began the countdown. The moment we were taping, my guest froze. Taking one finger out of his pocket, he literally pried his teeth from his lips—dry mouth being a common response to nervousness. During his dental workout, I filled in with information the association had sent me and limited my questions to those requiring a yes or no response. Slowly, he calmed down. Then I asked him a question he really cared about, "What is the prognosis for the local housing market?" And he talked a mile a minute. At the commercial break, he again adjusted his sunglasses and said, "Do you think I'd be good in television?"

Here's the point: When you tap into what people care about, the stories will come out. Nervous people forget their concerns to talk about their passions. Even the shyest people can come alive when discussing subjects they find interesting. In fact, often their passion will be so overwhelming that you'll find yourself getting excited, too. (Restrain yourself from signing up to play handbells, raise guide dogs, and learn to line dance all in the same week.)

THE OBSERVER/PARTICIPANT METHOD
OF COLLECTING STORIES

By attending functions that precede your presentation, you can pick up on an organization's stories and on the stories of individuals in a low-key way. Once, by sitting with conference attendees out in the hall, I struck up a conversation with a woman who had worked in the same school for 16 years. "In the beginning, all the kids were friends of my own children, so I got to know them that way," she told me. "But now I'm seeing their little sisters and brothers. I do so enjoy watching the children grow. It's a real treat when they come back to visit."

While that might sound meager to you, she was telling me the story of her industry. As an employee of the school system, she had shared an important source of joy. From the platform, I was able to share her comments—with permission—with the group. In effect, this sort of storytelling mirrors a group's feelings back to it. The result: A powerful interaction as group members get back in touch with what matters to *them*.

If you are asked to speak at a meal function, ask if you can skip sitting at the head table, where they usually put a presenter, and indicate you'd like to sit with the troops. You may pick up a wonderful story or two during the meal.

SPOTTING STORY PATTERNS

The more stories you hear and read, the better you will become at spotting and repeating the rhythms and patterns that make for great tales. As you listen to the stories all around you, ask yourself: What does this remind me of in my life? What similar experience have I had?

Perhaps the more important pattern you can spot isn't really a pattern after all, but a sense of drama. Eudora Welty explained this sense in her book *One Writer's Beginnings,* "My instinct—the dramatic instinct—was to lead me, eventually, on the right track for a storyteller: the *scene* was full of hints, pointers, suggestions, and promises of things to find out and know about human beings."

You, too, will find that sense of the dramatic, if you know to look for it. Once you do, you will find stories everywhere you go, and although one or two will cry out to you as obvious, don't overlook those that speak to you in more subtle tones. Robert Fish cautions, "While wildly dramatic and exciting stories are great, don't despair if you don't have any. What's more important is what you see in the stories. Superficial people can't see meaning in the Big Bang. Great storytellers see 'the universe in a grain of sand.'"

For example, at a party you overhear a man talk about a funny situation with his bug-phobic wife. Their daughter allowed her new pet rabbit to hop around the kitchen floor and neglected to clean up after the animal. Then the wife wandered into the kitchen. Without her glasses and in a panicked state, the wife thought the kitchen floor was covered with roaches. In response to his wife's screams, the husband came and found his wife frantically stomping on bunny poops.

That's his story, and it might bring back into your memory a time when your father awakened screaming in the night to announce he'd captured a flea in the act of biting him. It was a cracker crumb. Since cracker crumbs don't move and don't have legs, your mother never figured out why he was confused but . . . .

Now take this story and "see the universe" in it. Perhaps this story serves as a metaphor for how we view the world. Do we expect to be bitten by fleas in our own beds? Or do we chalk up life's irritations as results of the ever-fallible human condition? The choice is ours. Whatever you decided, look for repetitive themes and drama, and then go to your life for the variation.

SUMMARY

Your life is filled with stories, many of which you consider too insignificant to share. However, if you understand that that which is most personal is most universal, you will see the intrinsic value of all stories and open yourself to a great richness. Stories come from your past, your present, and other people. This chapter contains many ways to recall those stories from your past that have significance. By interviewing other people, you can flesh out your past and learn from the lives of others. You can find stories in your present by being a good observer.

EXERCISES

1. Work with a partner to discover and develop stories. Go through the exercises together in the section "Mining for Gold from Your Past."
2. Observe your friends when you socialize. What stories do they tell? Who is the best storyteller and why? Where do this person's stories come from?
3. Ask a friend who knows you well what stories they may remember about you.
4. Choose a person to interview for stories. Review the section on open-ended and close-ended questions. Be sure to start with open-ended questions and move to close-ended.
5. Observe one of the following situations: people at a park, people at a restaurant or airport, or a sporting event. Make up stories about people and what you see.

Finding Stories in Everyday Life

In the faces of men and women I see God, and in my own face in the glass, I find letters from God dropt in the street, and every one is sign'd by God's name . . .

Walt Whitman, "Song of Myself"

Every blade of grass has its Angel that bends over it and whispers, "Grow, grow."

The Talmud

Within every ordinary moment there are millions of miracles.

Flavia Weedn, *To Walk in Stardust*

All stories are family stories. Every tale must sound as if it's being spoken aloud, overheard.

Richard Peck, *Love and Death at the Mall*

. . . I believe that storytelling is crucial to humans for existence, that in very complex ways, it helps us to see our own lives with more clarity.

Robert Boswell *Writing for Your Life #2*, edited by Sybil Steinberg

LEARNING TO SEE WITH A STORYTELLER'S EYE

If you and I were to walk in a field of clover, I could find a four-leaf clover faster than you. In fact, give me a little time and I'll hand you a whole bouquet of them. Why? The clover doesn't magically grow four leaves when it sees me coming. What gives?

Growing up in a small town in southern Indiana, I amused myself by hunting for four-leaf clovers. At first, I found nothing. Then I had a paradigm shift, which means I found a new way of looking at the situation. I reasoned that four-leaf clovers should actually stick out of the crowd. After all, they are different. Once I knew that I was looking for the new pattern—the odd extra leaf—finding the clovers became easy.

The key to finding four-leaf clovers and stories is the same: Pay attention to the pattern.

THE PATTERN

The leaves of our story clover are characters, building action, and resolution. Another word for building action or growth is **drama.** We label a moment "dramatic" because it portends change and suggests action. Action builds as the characters move closer and farther from resolution. Our constant restlessness embraces the very nature of life. We breathe, exchanging stale air for fresh. We grow hungry, and move from gnawing need to satiety. We are born and we begin to learn, and that learning causes us to change our desires and expectations. The rhythm of life is always to step away from one state and to experience another.

Action is the movement between our states. Visualize the clichéd fight scene in which the good guy and the bad guy struggle on the edge of a cliff, and you'll see action at its simplest. Action can be either internal or external or both. When we struggle to come to a decision, action happens

internally. When we wrestle with the garage door because the
opener won't work, the action is external. When we argue
with our spouse, the action is both external—words and gestures—and internal—our feelings and emotions. Stories flourish whenever **characters**, **action**, and **growth** intersect.
Since life revolves around the changes forced upon us and the
changes we initiate, stories are all around us.

Look closely at any story and you'll be able to pick out
the interplay of characters, action, and growth. In the fairy
tale "Little Red Riding Hood," the characters include Little
Red Riding Hood, the wolf, the grandmother, and the woodsman. The building action involves the wolf's desire to eat Little Red Riding Hood. The solution comes in the guise of the
courageous woodsman.

A story entertains when the characters and the action
engage and distract us. A story educates when we identify
with the characters and action and the solution teaches us a
lesson. A story inspires when the interaction of characters,
action, and solution leave us on a higher plain.

THE HERO'S JOURNEY

Our need for stories springs in part from the soothing feeling
that comes as we recognize patterns. "Ah," we whisper, "I can
guess what comes next." The pattern of stories most familiar
and most beloved tells of the hero's journey. Indeed, the pattern has such ancient roots that tarot cards codify this message in the "Major Arcana."

The hero begins life as an innocent, blissfully unaware, a
Fool. Because he does not know to look for danger, because
he is free of guile, his face stays forever turned upward toward
the Sun, the source of all good. Poor Fool, he cannot see the
danger opening beneath his feet, and even if he could, he
could not choose another path, because this is his Destiny.

Danger comes as a series of challenges. These may be physical or mental. The Challenges force the Fool to give up the simple beliefs of his youth. Often, the Fool must come to grips with unpleasant Truths about himself. Finally, the Fool triumphs and grows in stature. This growth is heralded by Honors and Rewards.

You know this pattern. Consider *The Wizard of Oz*. The story begins when Dorothy's dog Toto bites the nasty spinster next door. Forced to flee to save Toto's life, Dorothy runs away from her family. Caught up in an emotional and physical storm, Dorothy finds herself in Oz, a strange land where challenges occur at every juncture. Dorothy meets one crisis after another, killing a witch, running from an enchanted forest, and gaining entrance to the great Wizard. The Wizard issues another challenge: Dorothy must face the Wicked Witch, a dead ringer for the nasty neighbor. Ultimately, Dorothy confronts her fears and takes courageous action against the Wicked Witch. Thus she learns her ticket home always existed—because her source of power was deep within herself. The final scenes show her being honored in Oz and then welcomed in Kansas.

Every hero—and Dorothy is but one—makes a similar journey. To become fully actualized humans we must leave home, confront the world and our fears, and return changed. Once we complete one cycle of the journey, we move on and spiral up to the next. Those who refuse the journey never grow, never truly come to peace with themselves, because they have decided instead to spend their lives as victims, locked into the *rake syndrome.* In the rake syndrome, you keep stepping on the same rake, hidden in the same pile of leaves, getting hit between the eyes over and over again.

Usually, what Heroes must confront is our own "fatal flaw," a deeply imbedded personal characteristic which makes us who we are—simultaneously extending and limiting our horizons. All our strengths, when overused, become our weaknesses. So we must be willing to examine those strengths rigorously, honestly, before we can move ahead. Dorothy's strength was a sweet nature, which also characterized her weakness, a dreaminess that reinforced a lack of personal initiative. After exhausting all other possibilities, after looking to the unlikeliest of saviors (a cowardly lion, a heartless tin man, and a brainless scarecrow), she was guided by a higher power (the Good Witch) to look within.

Certain life events force us to measure our progress and growth even if we never do leave Kansas. Society has rituals to mark these events, or rites of passage. Typical rites of passage include going to school, graduation, entrance into the work world, marriage, parenthood, the death of our own parents, the birthing and leaving of our children, our old age, and our death. Because these times represent milestones in our life, they often generate our most poignant stories.

As Jack Zipes says in *Creative Storytelling: Building Community, Changing Lives,* "The rites of passage are at the basis of most myths throughout the world." During these rites of passage, society acknowledges our growth, thus speeding us along as we create our own personal myths.

HOW SPEAKERS USE THE HERO'S JOURNEY

Dynamic, life-changing speakers help their audiences to travel the hero's journey by sharing their own stories. Conversely, an unprocessed story told from the platform falls flat. The circuit is not complete and the electricity can't connect. But when we process our lives, or as Grady Jim Robinson says, "mythologize" them, we move from petty disappointments to grander scales. As George Bernard Shaw said, "This is the true joy in life, the being used for a purpose recognized by yourself as a mighty one . . . the being a force of nature

instead of a feverish, selfish little clod of ailments and griev-
ances complaining that the world will not devote itself to
making you happy." By sharing our growth, we become that
force of nature, inviting our listeners to consider their own
journeys and their personal progress.

Therefore, to be effective, you must process the story by
seeing the humor and the growth in what happened. Each
story you tell must show the listener how to complete the
journey, and it must include an element of personal discovery
and responsibility. In the final analysis, the story must tell
how you arrived on higher ground. Which also means you
must reveal, somewhere and somehow in the story, that you
have been vulnerable. Otherwise there is no chance for
growth. This vulnerability becomes a stumbling block for
many speakers who see the platform as a place to reinforce
personal grandeur rather than share personal growth. Yet, con-
necting with an audience, closing the gap between the platform and their hearts can only happen when we are open and
vulnerable. This vulnerability becomes our gift to the people
who've allowed us to take up their time with our stories.

We can only process our stories when we embrace them.
Psychologists know the greatest obstacle to human growth is
denial. But, when we embrace who we are and the totality of
our experience, we accept our flaws. Then and only then are
we open to the possibility of moving ahead.

"In fact, each stage (of the hero's journey) has a gift for
us, something critical to teach us about being human,"
explains Carol S. Pearson in *The Hero Within*. You don't grow
from perfect; you grow from human. If your presentation
doesn't share your growth, you fail to deliver the hope. The
world is filled with sorrows and disappointments. You have
no right to add to your audiences' burdens. But you do have
a responsibility to become a life changer. As Grady Jim Robinson explains, "Every human being suffers childhood wounds

that are real that you deal with today. As a speaker you have an obligation to dig down into your heart, your mind, and your soul and touch wounds of your life, process them, deal with them and then lay them out there for your audiences so that their lives can change."

BE WILLING TO LET STORIES DEVELOP

Poor Zeus, king of the Greek gods, suffered with a pounding headache. Seeing his agony, Hephaestus, god of fire, grabbed his tools and split open Zeus's head. Athena sprang fully grown from her father's skull.

If only stories would spring fully grown from our heads!

When asked how he came to write his hit song "Valotte," Julian Lennon said, "The song came to me all at once." On occasion, a story will show up, dressed to the hilt and ready to party. More often, stories appear as seedlings and we must tend them like faithful gardeners if they are ever to bear fruit.

In *The Ageless Spirit,* Philip Berman and Connie Goldman tell of how writer and director Norman Corwin saw poet Carl Sandburg pulling scraps of paper out of his pocket. The papers contained scraps of poems, a few of which Corwin recognized as gems. Corwin asked Sandburg why he hadn't published this handful of poems, and Sandburg said, "Because I'm not through with them."

Pianist Van Cliburn has tapes of his performances in the vaults of recording companies. When asked why he hasn't released them, he has said, "I have always taken the long view of my career." The implication is that these pieces are not available for public consumption because Cliburn is not through with them.

One speaker who puts a great deal of time and effort into her stories is Patricia Fripp, the first woman president of the National Speakers Association. "After all," says Fripp, "you can use a good story for years." Grady Jim Robinson is another speaker who admits to having worked on some of his stories for years.

Fortunately for most speakers, we can release our material before it is fully formed and watch it grow. Even if you are speaking to create product and your speech will go on tape to be distributed forever, you can continue to work on and improve your material each time you present. In this way, good speakers "cheat yesterday's audience," as Mark Sanborn explains, by always improving our presentations.

SUMMARY

All stories follow similar patterns of drama with characters, building action, and resolution. Once you learn to spot these elements, finding stories becomes easy. The "hero's journey" offers one way to see the difference between interesting stories and those with lasting value. To complete the journey, the hero must travel from innocence to tragedy and grow into maturation, accepting his or her flaws and moving on with a new perspective. Stories do not always develop quickly or easily, so be prepared to work with them.

EXERCISES

1. Take a fairy tale, a movie, and a novel and point out the characters, building action, and resolution.
2. Find a story that fits the "hero's journey" mold. Tell your class or your story partner about this story and why it signifies personal growth.

6 Shaping the Stories

We are to enter into our depths, our ground, our mystery and hiddenness, and work from there.

Matthew Fox, *The Reinvention of Work*

Memorable eloquence is comprised of four elements: great man (or woman), great occasion, great words, and great delivery.

James C. Humes, *Standing Ovation*

Say that you are telling a story to children. You instinctively tell it, change it, adapt it, cut it, expand it, all under their large, listening eyes, so that they will be arrested and held by it throughout.

Brenda Ueland, *If You Want to Write*

CRAFTING THE STORY

Every summer of my childhood, I would spend a week at Girl Scout camp at Camp Wildwood in Vincennes, Indiana. Next to eating S'Mores and sloppy Joes, the best part of camp was arts and crafts. Armed with tongue depressors, glue, poster paint, and sparkles, we made amazing gifts for our families: picture frames, bird houses, pencil cups, and note-paper holders. In the heat of the day, our heads bent over our projects, our chubby fingers pushing and poking and holding our work together. Every so often, we'd look longingly at the sample before us. Inspired, we'd return our full attention to the project at hand.

Crafting a story requires the same concentration, patience, and vision. And you do get your fingers stuck together once in a while as you try to decipher your thoughts. But, just as in my scouting days, you can follow patterns and arrange pieces to create a masterpiece. Crafting a story is a skill you can learn by attacking your work one piece at a time.

KEY ELEMENTS

At scout camp, the arts and crafts instructor would first make sure we each had all the pieces we needed to make our masterpiece. Good stories always share the same key elements, pieces that are common to every good tale.

- Build-up, or background information, including character development
- Action, or building of conflict
- Climax, which is discovery, decision, or conflict
- Punch line, punch word, or trigger word
- *Dénouement* or resolution

You can start your story crafting with any of the above pieces.

1. Build-Up or Background Information, and Character Development

Character and background information can bring back old stories you've forgotten or turn a simple scenario into a memorable scene. One speaker's favorite keynote story jelled when he was walking behind a group of Scottish people in O'Hare airport. He had been noodling around a story about falling off a horse, and suddenly the groomsman in his story came to life as he mentally gave that character a Scottish accent.

The attention your audience gives a character will be directly proportional to how sympathetic that character is. Many a bad plot has been rescued by a sympathetic character, and many a good plot has been ruined by a character whom no one cared about.

TIP *Don't misinterpret the term* sympathetic. *You don't have to feel sorry for a character to connect with him or her. Ethan Canin once told Anne Lamotte, "Nothing is as important as a likable narrator. Nothing holds a story together better." We may laugh at the narrator's problems, we may consider her morals to be sleazy, but if she doesn't hold our interest, we'll opt out of her story.*

When speaking, you are the narrator. If you are not likable, your audience will tune you out. This was vividly illustrated when a well-known speaker started name dropping his way through his presentation. Every other phrase was, "So the president of IBM asked me," or, "After I returned the call from Sony's chairman." Within seconds, the crowd grew agitated. They wondered what he was trying to prove. Whatever it was, his pomposity did not engage the audience's affections.

What makes a narrator unlikable? Arrogance. Pomposity. Invulnerability. Lack of growth. When a character makes the same mistake over and over, the listener wants to scream, "Enough already! Get a life! Move on and quit wasting my time."

We don't want or expect narrators to be perfect. In fact, we love people for their warts, not despite them. Being human and real works. Being vulnerable works. Being an egotist or a victim doesn't.

TIP *A good background alone can entice your listener into your story. When you think about background, comb your mind for places you've lived in or visited. A background of a golf hole at Mauna Kea, Hawaii, brings to mind the crashing of the surf against the volcanic rock echoed by the swinging slap of clubs against golf balls. Sounds like a terrific beginning for a story, doesn't it?*

You will also want to consider *foreshadowing.* Information about the past is called *clues,* whereas information about the future is called *foreshadowing.* As you craft your story, you use foreshadowing to suggest what is ahead. Ever notice how a movie will use scary music to signal the villain's approach? The scary music foreshadows an evil deed. Remember the movie *Jaws?* Before the shark would appear, the music would signal his presence. By midway through the movie, the playing of the theme caused people to cover their eyes and whisper, "I can't look!"

In Cold Blood, by Truman Capote, exemplifies the tremendous tension created by a storyteller who is a master of foreshadowing. Over and over, Capote details the mundane life of a simple family and adds that they are going about these daily activities for the last time. With only the slightest hint, he signals to the reader that these people are about to be killed. More recently, Elizabeth George began her book *For the Sake of Elena* with a sympathetic rendering of a morning in the life of a woman. George limited her foreshadowing to one chilling sentence: "And she had less than fifteen minutes to live."

You don't have to tell about a murder to use foreshadowing. You can tell of a situation in a straightforward manner and then give a tiny twist, a quick turning along the path you've trodden.

See if you can spot the foreshadowing in the story that follows:

When Mary checked into the hotel, she immediately called her cotrainer, Alfred, from her room.

"Do you know how to get to the training site at the factory?" she asked.

"Yeh, yeh. I've been there a dozen times. I even brought a map and got directions."

The two agreed to meet the next morning at 6 A.M. for breakfast and then said goodnight. Mary worried, thinking back to other trips with Al. His definition of *directions* and hers were quite different. Then she turned on the weather channel, "Sleet . . . turning to icy rain . . . ."

The next morning after breakfast, as they lugged boxes of books, handouts, and flipcharts to the car Al had rented, Al handed Mary a poorly copied map from the rental car agency. At each major intersection, the huge logo of the rental car agency, designating a drop-off site, covered the street names. On the right-hand margin were scribbled a few unreadable notes. As they pulled out of the parking lot, big icy glops of rain pelted the windshield.

"Al, aren't we going the wrong way?" asked Mary.

"Nope. This is the way I came in," he said, slurping his coffee.

"But the factory is south and we're going north," said Mary. They continued on through two toll booths. The signs ahead said "Milwaukee." Mary asked the third toll booth agent, "Where is Rosemont?" And the gray-haired attendant laughed. "About an hour the other direction."

Al turned around. They drove slowly through the stop-and-go traffic congested around O'Hare. The car wheels spun in the gathering sleet. "We're gonna be late!" he bellowed, and he began to pound his fist on the steering wheel. Mary sat terrified in the passenger's seat, trying to recall her Lamaze breathing.

Then Al broke the silence with a news flash: "Throw another log on the fire. We're out of gas!"

Notice the ways the crisis builds in this vignette. Mary's concerns are surfaced early in the story. The mounting weather problem adds to the drama. You know the resolution will not be pretty.

By using foreshadowing, you can build tension and drama into a story that will keep your audience involved even if the story does not have a lot of action. When the story has a lot of action, foreshadowing builds the action and creates a greater final impact. In the story of "The Three Little Pigs," the repeated threats and visits of the wolf to the pig's houses add impact to the story's climax and keep the story interesting.

How do you create foreshadowing? Working backward works best. Look at the end result and go back to plant clues in the early part of your story.

2. Action, or Building of Conflict

Here we search for the motion that drives the story forward. Ask yourself:

- ▪ What happened next?
- ▪ What did I see or hear or smell or taste or feel or notice?
- ▪ What was my major character doing?

The action in the story of Mary and Al comes as the weather worsens and the time trickles away.

Action does not have to be physical. We mentally move forward when we conquer a problem or make a discovery. Words that show mental action include *showed, created, thought, decided, felt, concluded, spotted, examined, discovered, admitted, found, realized, shared, tried, avoided, helped, determined,* and *confronted.*

3. Climax

The climax of any story refers to the apex of the action. If you visualize a story as a roller coaster, the background builds as the cars chug their way up the first hill, the foreshadowing happens as you hesitate at the top of the hill and see the hills and dips ahead, and the climax is the first sensation of leaving your seat as your car goes hurtling down the rails, dropping down . . . down . . . down into space.

In the climax, everything comes to a head. All heck breaks loose. But the climax won't work if the story is unbelievable. A story in which the hand of God reaches down and plucks the character out of the dilemma won't be satisfying. The audience wants to see or hear how the character has grown and responds to the difficult situation.

In the movie *Thelma and Louise,* the climax came in the last moments of the movie. The ending was incredibly exciting because just as it seemed that the two characters had run out of options, they invented a new—and horrifying—option for themselves.

Not all climaxes will be so thrilling. But, each climax must, however briefly, hold the heart of the audience in your hand to be satisfying.

4. Punch Line, Punch Word, or Trigger Word

Although *punch line* generally refers to the climax of a joke, any sentence or phrase that delivers the climax of a story could be called a punch line. To determine which sentence or phrase is the punch line, simply leave the sentence or phrase out and see what happens. Without the punch line, the material that preceded it makes no sense.

The punch line offers the speaker and the listener the chance to experience what James Joyce called an epiphany, or a crisis of thought which, once resolved, forever changes those involved. These mental conversions lead our listeners through the growth we have experienced, allow them to share the experience, and punctuate the revelation with an "Aha!"

In *Thelma and Louise,* there was no punch line or word, but a look passes between the two characters and then they take a "punch action," driving their car off a cliff.

5. Dénouement

This French word, *dénouement,* literally means "unknotting." The dénouement brings us to the resolution of the situation. The conflict comes to its inevitable conclusion, and all is well. In spoken short stories, this segment may be brief or practically nonexistent.

A useful illustration for a story is the inverted checkmark (see Figure 6.1). Here you can see how the parts of the story build to the climax. The resolution serves to help satisfy the audience.

Figure 6.1

THE SHAPE OF A STORY

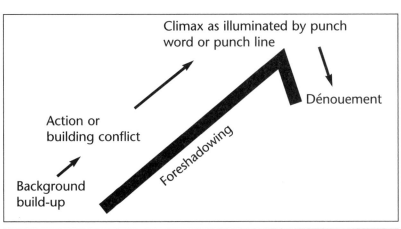

OTHER STORY CONSIDERATIONS

A great story becomes one of the many elements that must coexist within your presentation. Unless you are telling the story of your life in narrative form, you will need to position the story properly within the presentation for maximum impact.

A myriad of story considerations determines the overall shape and flavor of our finished presentation. When you have trouble making a story fit, trouble taming a rambling episode, or trouble making your point, you have probably ignored one of these considerations. By playing with these elements, you can discover the best placement and setting for your story.

1. Voice

Who tells the story? Do you, as the speaker, narrate the story? If so, the story will be told in first person and probably in the order of events as they happened. Example: "I woke up and saw the alarm and then I . . . ."

Another choice would shift the I–You Ratio by letting another character tell the story in the third person. This allows the speaker to comment on the story and to rearrange the time sequence.

> Example: "My friend Jennifer told me about her most embarrassing moment. *She doesn't seem like a forgetful sort of person, but how anyone could lose her car for three hours escapes me.* Here's what she did . . . " The italics show the section where the speaker makes a comment.

2. Persona

Will you tell the story as yourself, or will you become a character? A handful of speakers dress, talk, and act like famous people from the past. Gene Griessman becomes Abraham Lincoln. Ralph Archbold becomes Ben Franklin. Mary Beth Roach becomes Mae West.

You don't have to go that far. Liz Curtis Higgs calls herself a "big beautiful woman in a narrow nervous world." Alyce Cornyn-Selby bills herself as the *War Bride*. The persona you adapt grows from the impression you project on stage. *Persona* comes from the Greek term for mask. We all wear masks, and on the platform, the mask extends and exaggerates our natural selves. For seriousness, make sure your persona and you project a coherent message. To project humor, play up the disparity between your persona and other aspects of your life.

3. Pace

While in his 90s, the great statistician and teacher Dr. W. Edwards Deming still appeared in person to lecture on the subject of total quality management. The seminar Deming taught businesspeople lasted four days. The first day, the students were star-struck to hear and see the great man who taught the Japanese a revolutionary way of producing high-quality products. The excitement died down by the middle of the afternoon. By three o'clock, heads were nodding all over the lecture hall. Here and there a "thunk" sounded as pens dropped from the hands of snoozing students. As a statistician, Deming was a genius. As a presenter, he left a lot to be desired. The greatest problem was the monotony of his vocal range and his metronome-like pace; he had the rhythm and range of a grandfather clock between chimes.

Now, unless you are as world-renowned as Ed Deming, you better operate on variable speeds. Within and without stories, you must speed up, slow down, and add variety. A simple rule is to slow down as you get to your punch line. When speeding up, be careful. Many speakers talk so quickly that the audience misses the point. Remember: When we are nervous and excited—and the platform is an exhilarating place—we naturally speed up. Vary your rate, but realize that your concept of speed and the audience's may be vastly different.

4. Graph

Once you have put together an entire presentation, you need to graph the emotional highs and lows. Naomi Rhode suggests graphing as a way to examine visually the emotional flow of your commentary.

Simply outline your presentation, noting the stories or exercises you will feature. Then go back and add plus signs (+) for upbeat sections and minus signs (–) for downbeat sections. Then look at the overall pattern. The audience cannot sustain feelings of sadness or unhappiness for too long. You must mix in a healthy dollop of hope and humor.

You may wish to do this by making sure your stories mythologize the protagonist. Bring the situation full circle and show your audience the learning that took place.

TIP *Never end a presentation with a depressing story that does not offer the audience hope. You may want to use a tear jerker as the next to the last story or piece and then immediately follow with an upper.*

Some speakers have said that when you end on a negative note, you will not get a standing ovation. Standing ovations are overrated; but then, so are chocolate, sex, love, and money. If your goal is to impress the audience, you need to rethink why you want to speak.

Here is a terrific poem by Mark Sanborn that first appeared in *What to Say When . . . You're Dying on the Platform* by Lilly Walters. It might change the way you view a standing ovation.

I Didn't Get a Standing Ovation Today

I didn't get a standing ovation today,
But I learned afterwards a woman in the front row with
    cancer
Nodded in agreement as I spoke of overcoming a
    circumstance.

I didn't get a standing ovation a week ago,
But a small group stayed late after the program.
They bought the beer and we shared great stories.

I didn't get a standing ovation a month ago,
But a manager from that program sent me a note.
He said my presentation encouraged him to keep trying.

I did get a standing ovation recently,
I gave a pretty good speech, but after the applause,
I don't remember much else that was remarkable that day.

I didn't get a standing ovation today,
Instead, somehow I connected with the human spirit.

5. Repetitive Theme or Golden Thread

A repetitive theme is an idea that echoes throughout a presentation, while a golden thread may be a specific phrase that
is repeated for emphasis. When a humorous situation reap-
pears in a presentation, it is termed a *callback,* or, more commonly, a *running joke.* Trainer Ellen Dowling says in her book
The Standup Trainer, "The rule for a callback is this: The bit
must get a laugh the first time."

In a presentation for the National Speakers Association,
Lou Heckler explained how a repetitive theme can help an
audience feel a sense of closure. He cited a presentation given

by Erma Bombeck. As she walked to the platform, Bombeck made a little gesture with her hand to lick and plaster down a piece of her hair. The gesture may have been totally spontaneous and informal, but it spoke volumes about her personal authenticity. In a nonverbal way, the gesture suggested a theme for Bombeck's presentation: I am a real person like you. At the end of her presentation, Bombeck again repeated the gesture. The piece, taken as a whole with the nonverbal and the verbal themes matching each other, gave the audience a feeling of closure.

Emory Austin uses her parents' admonition, "What would an extraordinary person do?" as a golden thread. Austin introduces the idea early in her presentation. Then, she repeats the question in each segment of her speech. As a result, the listener understands the abiding impact of her parents' values while hearing how they guided Austin through her life.

Patricia Fripp uses a golden thread to highlight irony in her keynote *How to Be an Overnight Success*. Early on, she notes that people have often called her an overnight success; then she adds, "And it only took me 15 years." The theme of the keynote revolves around the hard work and dedication Fripp brings to her craft. At various times throughout, Fripp repeats, "And it only took me 15 years." This way, she subtly laughs at the idea that success comes easily or without hard work.

6. Circular Construction

Circular construction occurs on a grand scale and on a small scale to give the listener a sense of closure. You have seen and heard this device used throughout your life, although often it occurs so subtly that you may not have been aware of its presence. In circular construction, the story always comes back to an element introduced in its beginning. The Book of

Genesis sets up and repeats a circular rhythm over and over with, "And God called . . . And God made . . . And God said." The story of "The Three Little Pigs" begins with the pigs leaving home, reaches high drama with the destruction of their homes, and concludes with a party at the home of the eldest porker. *The Wizard of Oz* begins with Dorothy running away from home and ends with her returning home. *Gone with the Wind* begins with Mr. O'Hara telling his daughter, "Tara is in your blood, Katie Scarlett," and concludes the first half as Scarlett O'Hara stands before a silhouette of Tara.

The following is an example of a speech that uses circular construction:

> I grew up in a little town called Vincennes, Indiana, but my mother's mother, my grandmother, lived in South Carolina. So every summer, my mother would put my sisters and me in the car, and we would make the long trip from Indiana down to South Carolina. To me that trip was the most exciting time of my life. We got up so early it was before the sun came up. It was still dark outside. The dew was on the grass. The crickets were singing. I loved the way there was nothing in the world till our headlights hit it. And then out of nothing would come a tree, a house, an animal by the side of the road. It was magic to me the way the sky turned from inky black to gray, and then streaked with peach and lavender, and finally to the warm yellow of the sun. It seemed to me life was so full of potential and anything was possible. So in my mind, I gave those mornings a name. I called them South Carolina Mornings. [The presentation continues . . . and then ends with:]
>
> I woke up early. It was dark outside. I said goodbye to my sleeping second husband. I went in and planted a kiss on the cheek of my four-year-old son. I got in the car to go speak for a living. It was dark outside, but you know when the headlights hit things suddenly a house would appear and a dog and a tree. And the sky

was inky black. But, then it turned to gray, and it was streaked with lavender and peach. And suddenly the warmth, the sun filled me, and it was a South Carolina Morning all over again.

As you can see, the sunrise performed double-duty. Sunrises signal new beginnings, and in my presentation they also signaled renewed joy in my life. Because colorations are mentioned, audiences can use the hues to help stir their imaginations.

7. Audience Participation

A story can set the stage to allow the audience to participate and join in the fun. Audience participation always raises the energy level of the group while demanding its total attention.

Lou Heckler is a master of audience participation on a variety of levels. He uses stories and elements within presentations to lock concepts into the minds of listeners. He builds into his presentations a sense of spontaneity that allows the audience to play. Once, while presenting to the National Speakers Association (NSA), he asked the group to take a pledge. "Repeat after me," he said. "I, state your name, do solemnly swear . . . " The audience repeated his comments word for word, including "state your name" instead of inserting their own names!

After teasing the audience about its confusion, Heckler built on the situation. He noted that in the South, when a person makes an obvious and silly mistake, other people will murmur, "Bless your heart." Heckler explains that "Bless your heart" is not really a blessing, but a subtle way of saying, "Gee, how dumb can you get?"

Now . . . he's set the stage. Heckler invites the audience to shout out, "Bless your heart!" when he says anything dumb. And they do!

Note that although Heckler has not told a full-blown story, he has created a story by involving the audience. If you had been present at that session—and his sessions are always standing room only—you would have left dying to tell your friends about what happened. Note, too, that all the classical story elements are here. First, we have the build-up or background (asking people to take the pledge), then the climax (people "tricked" into saying "state your name"), and finally the resolution (an explanation that Southerners might handle this by saying "Bless your heart"). The callback occurs when an audience member shouts, "Bless your heart!" during the course of the presentation.

Humorist Karyn Buxman sets up audience participation by asking the group to stand and give themselves a standing ovation. Then she suggests that if an individual feels the need for more recognition in his or her life, he or she can pop up during her presentation and ask for a standing ovation. This has worked well for her, incorporating a sense of fun and spontaneity into her presentations on humor. In addition, this audience participation has offered her a new anecdote. During one presentation, a woman in the back of the group leaped to her feet, threw her arms up into the air and shouted, "I need a tubal ligation!" Imagine the audience reaction to that piece of news!

TIP *The longer your presentation is, the more time you should consider setting aside for audience participation. Because of the amount of time they spend before audiences, and because of the need to make sure people retain new information, trainers master audience participation early in their careers. Conversely, keynoters may tend to ignore participation because keynotes tend to be short, entertainment-dense, and centered around the presenter. All speakers can improve their impact by using participation techniques.*

Levels of audience participation vary:

- **Level 1**—Ask them to get involved on an internal level: "Have you ever considered how many sunrises you will see in your entire life?"
- **Level 2**—Get them involved on a simple, external level. You might ask them to hold up their hands in response to a simple question, such as "How many of you have ever been to Peoria, Illinois?"
- **Level 3**—Ask them to do something physical that does not involve another person: "Please cross your legs, one over the over."
- **Level 4**—Ask them to talk to another person: "Tell the person next to you your name."
- **Level 5**—Ask them to get up and move: "Please walk to the back of the room."
- **Level 6**—Ask them to play a game or work on a project: "Please take a piece of paper and a crayon, get together in groups, and draw a picture of your work place."

As you can tell, the stakes go up with each level of involvement. At each level, you ask a little more of your audience, and it may feel a greater level of risk. There are two ways to offset the risk: (1) explain why you are asking this of them, and (2) laugh with them about how they might feel ("I know, don't you hate it when the speaker asks you to move? Gee! And you spent so much time picking the exact chair you wanted."). Most people will move reluctantly, but once they get involved, regaining their attention can be tough because people love to be involved with each other!

Many speakers and presenters shy away from interaction because they fear losing control of the group. That's a shame. We have no control over our groups. Ever. We are always at the mercy of their goodwill, and we would do well not to forget that. Higher interaction guarantees higher involvement and always improves your evaluations as a speaker.

ESSENTIALS FOR CRAFTING A TERRIFIC STORY

1. KISS: Keep It Short and Simple

Robert Fish believes that if most people cut 10 to 20 percent off their stories, they would improve them dramatically. This would mean cutting 1 to 2 minutes off a 10-minute story and 30 seconds to 1 minute off a 5-minute story.

Pare your stories to the bone. Chart out the essentials and then rebuild. A few quick rules:

- The length of the story should be commensurate with its impact. In other words, the longer the story, the more impact it should have. The shorter the story, the less impact it must have.
- The longer the story, the more characters it can support.
- The shorter the story, the more the pace of your presentation will pick up.

TIP *Challenge every word in your story. Ask yourself, "What happens if I leave this out?" Every word and every part of the story must move the action along. If it doesn't, it's deadwood. Trash it.*

2. Use Significant Detail

William Zinsser calls this "visible detail." We come to know and understand the world around us through our five senses. Good speakers engage our senses to force listeners to step into the world of the story. Barry Mann says, "The details I bring in, while not essential to the development of the conflict, are essential to giving the listeners something to respond to, to hang their emotions on." Think of your story as a room and significant details as the doors into the room.

The following is an example of a sentence lacking significant detail:

She was sitting in a rocking chair knitting socks.

Now, let's add the details:

My grandmother was sitting in the oak rocker knitting a small pair of robin's egg blue socks.

By changing the significant detail, we change the picture in the listener's mind. Try this:

My sister was sitting in the wicker rocker knitting a green and red scarf.

In each of the three sentences a female sits in a rocking chair and knits, but when the significant details have changed, the pictures have changed in your mind.

TIP *Review each story you tell for ways to involve the five senses. Then, look at each story and consider what the scene looked like. Finally, ask yourself how you can better develop each character by using significant detail.*

A terrific way to develop a character is to share quirky details about the person. When I talk about my maternal grandmother, I tell about her blue Keds tennis shoes which she stuffed with cotton to pad the amputated stumps of her toes and about her clip-on sunglasses.

Imagine these different characters:

- a man wearing a white t-shirt with a pack of Camels rolled up in one sleeve
- a pregnant teenager flicking her ponytail back and forth between her fingers as she fills out a job application and rolling a piece of peppermint gum around her mouth
- an elderly man as pale and bleached out as a dry sand dollar, balancing his weight on a stainless steel cane, and

shading his eyes with his palm so he can look up and read a storefront sign

With a little imagination, you could spin yarns about all their lives based on the snippets of information you were given.

3. Show, Don't Tell

By nature, people today are highly skeptical. When you tell the audience what happened, they can choose whether or not to be involved. When you show the audience what happened, audience members have the opportunity to come to their own conclusions. Think about your own life. Your parents can tell you why you should save money, but until that day that you need money and you don't have any, the lesson has little impact. I can tell you the man's appearance frightened me, or I can say, "He was about six feet five inches tall, weighed about 280 pounds, and walked like a grizzly bear who just woke up. Under his left eye ran a long jagged scar. Wrapped around his left fist was a thick, chrome chain. He headed straight for me." Now that I've filled you in on the details, your mental dialogue is probably saying, "Geez, I would be scared, too!" But when I simply tell you "his appearance frightened me," you ask yourself, "Why?" And while you pause to wonder, you have missed the next part of my presentation.

You *show* what happened by creating a mood, sharing details, and telling what was observed. Because you and I are two different people, we can observe a situation and walk away with different impressions. The speaker controls or shapes the audience's reaction by carefully choosing what to share. Therefore, the more you tell a story, the more input you receive from your listeners, the better you can shape your story to fit your objectives.

TIP *A legendary trainer counsels that a good presenter tells his or her audiences "1, 2, 3, 4, 5, 6, 7, 8, ____, 10" and lets them fill in the 9. Barry Mann suggests, "Let people fill in some of your story, so that it becomes their story."*

When we tell, rather than show, we rob our audiences of the joy of discovery. By inviting our listeners to discover truths for themselves, we help them stay involved in our presentation. The best evaluations come from audiences who felt like they were part of the presentation.

4. Plan for a Variety of Characters

If in one story your protagonist is a woman, you might consider using a male protagonist in your next story. By varying the gender of your characters, you give all audience members a chance to see themselves in the stories you share.

Audiences look at speakers and make startling assumptions about who they are and where they are coming from. Because they make leaps based on what they think they see, a wonderful way to use stories involves playing people's expectations against realities. When I was copresenting with empowerment expert Michael Scott on the topic of communications, we talked about how to deal with a crying employee. Scott is African American, and he began his remarks by saying, "Culture plays an important part in understanding other people, and especially in understanding why another person might react to a tough situation by crying." Of course, the group thought Scott was going to share how African Americans react to crying. Instead, he told a story of supervising a Hispanic gentleman whose work performance and attendance had suddenly become shoddy. When pressed on the matter, the Hispanic man explained that he had a family member who was ill, and through tears he told Scott, "You are being insensitive to our culture. You don't understand that to us family has first priority."

By sharing this story, Scott reminded the group that our country is a melting pot of many cultures and that we must all work to understand each other. Scott deftly showed the group that he, too, had to learn to communicate with others of differing backgrounds.

By asking Scott to assist me with my presentation, and by his inclusion of his story about a Hispanic person, we managed to represent a broader spectrum of humanity.

TIP *Review your stories. Ask yourself:*

- What are the ages of my characters?
- What is their racial background?
- What is their religious background?
- What is their gender?
- What are their occupations?

Concentrate on creating a multiplicity of characters in your stories. Be sure that the villains of your stories are not all from the same background.

TIP *Business audiences tend to tune you out if they don't sense a strong business slant to your presentation— unless, of course, you were hired specifically to talk about a personal or family issue. If you are speaking to a business audience, you may want your lead anecdote to be about a businessperson in a business dilemma. As your presentation continues, you can weave in stories about yourself and about families. Business audiences also react positively if you start with information about a person who is a leader in that particular industry.*

5. Use Dialects, Vocal Variety, Changes in Volume, and Stage Placement to Build Characters

When telling a story involving several characters, moving from character to character can become quite tedious if you repeat, "He said, she said," over and over. Instead, shift from character to character by using dialects, vocal variety, changes in volume, and stage placement.

Dialects and Accents

Using dialects or accents for different characters gives significant detail and distinguishes one character from another. Success springs from using a dialect or accent subtly. Don't try to sound like a Frenchman straight from the streets of Paris, but do practice a hint of an accent. If you put on too thick of an accent, no one will understand you and the audience will get so caught up in trying to figure out what you are saying that it won't be able to follow your drift. Just suggest the accent. Tape recording a native speaker offers the best way to mimic an accent. Find a person who has an interesting accent, ask that person to tape record the dialogue you want to use, listen to the tape, and try to reproduce what you hear. It's okay if your reproduction isn't perfect; Meryl Streep doesn't need the competition. Remember, your goal is to delineate characters, not win an Academy Award.

Of course, be sensitive to stereotyping and making fun of other cultures when you use a dialect. The best course is to assign a dialogue to a person whose behavior in the situation is either obviously positive or entirely neutral. Choosing to poke fun only at your own nationality—as long as the audience realizes what that nationality is—offers another safeguard. When speaker Frank Bucaro puts on his best Sicilian godfather accent and talks about the Family, the audience absolves Bucaro of all sins because Bucaro has told them beforehand that he is Sicilian. Make sure the audience knows who you are and where you are coming from when you laugh at yourself.

Vocal Variety

Without resorting to dialects or accents, you can create a multiplicity of characters by changing the pitch and speed of your voice. Pitch reflects how high or low your voice is. Timbre, according to Patricia Ball in her book *Straight Talk Is More Than Words*, "is a voice's changing qualities: softness, smoothness, brittleness." The speed of your voice measures how fast you talk. Ball notes that "an effective rate of speech is between one-hundred-forty and one-hundred-sixty words per minute."

For the finest example of the impact of vocal variety, listen to books on tape: You'll quickly note how one actor can create an entire cast of characters. Hearing professionals use their voices to create such distinctions will give you new ideas to try as a speaker.

As a simple way to practice vocal variety, read aloud to a child. Create different voices for "The Three Billy Goats Gruff," with baby goat speaking in a wispy little voice, the middle goat using your natural voice, and the big brother tapping all the bass you can muster. Don't forget to find a totally weird voice inside you to play the part of the troll that lives under the bridge.

TIP *Books on tape are a great boon to speakers. Besides teaching vocal variety, the art of the pause, and storytelling, they provide great comfort and companionship to speakers traveling between engagements. While making a six-hour drive, one friend became so engrossed in a book on tape that she almost ran out of gas. Books on tape can be rented from your public library and some grocery stores.*

Volume

By switching from loud to soft, you can develop characters and build dramatic intensity. Oddly enough, the quieter you are, the more your audience is forced to listen to you. Certainly, you don't want to speak so quietly that you can't be heard. But do experiment with dropping your volume. On the other hand, by adding a dimension of volume, you can distinguish forceful characters from those who are more subtle.

Stage Placement

By moving from one stage location to another, you can create more than one person. You "plant" a person on one spot on the stage. Decide where the character will be and speak in the character's voice from that spot. Then, step to another spot to assume the identity of a second person. Make sure that you don't speak—as one character or the other—until you are in place. (Getting from one spot to the other, even if only inches define the shift, can seem like it takes forever. Trust your audience to stay with you. They will.)

As a variation of this, you position your body one way to be one person and then assume another position to be the second person. In the character of a witch, you might assume a crumpled up position. Shifting to the person of the beautiful maiden, you would stand up straight and tall.

As simplistic as this sounds, placement and posture define character quite well as long as you remember to assume the new character before you shift from being one person to another. Lou Heckler even uses placement and hand gestures to guide audiences through side commentaries. He introduces the comment and gestures with both hands in a sort of "hold that thought" way, and then moves across the stage where he picks up a new idea. At the completion of the new idea, he returns physically to the site of the "hold that thought" gesture, repeats it and continues the original story thread.

6. Rely on Strong Verbs

Vigorous verbs add action to your stories. Weak construction occurs when the speaker relies on adjectives and adverbs to paint word pictures. Strong verbs describing clear actions shorten sentences and force crystal clear images to pop into the brain.

For example, think about "Mary walked slowly into the hallway." By using a vigorous verb, you can shade the sentence much more precisely: "Mary meandered into the hallway." "Mary sauntered through the hallway." "Mary ambled through the hallway." Note how with each change of verb, you see a different motion and get a different feel for Mary.

The most delightful verbs linger in our minds because they are perfect and surprising. When a speaker selects verbs such as *roost, fidget, dawdle, finagle, explode, satisfy,* and *err,* that part of us that thrills to the largesse of the English language feasts on the banquet before us. At this writing, the English language encompasses six hundred and fifty thousand words and is growing at the phenomenal rate of five hundred words a year. How sad that many of us wear our small vocabularies out and our listeners' patience to shreds instead of conquering new words!

7. Use the Active Voice

Passive voice obscures the action and the actor, as well as lengthens the sentence. In passive construction, the doer and the deed are veiled by the addition of unnecessary words and convolution of the natural subject–verb construction. Active voice simplifies the thought by asking, "Who did what?" By design, it is straightforward and without pretense or prevarication.

The following are examples of the two voices:

Passive: The ball was thrown by the boy.

Active: The boy threw the ball.

Note how much shorter and cleaner active voice is. Whenever possible, tell your stories in active voice.

TIP *Remember: People listen and comprehend at differing rates. If your sentences get too long or too complex, your point becomes lost. As the listener struggles to figure out what you are saying, you move on, leaving your poor listener like a tourist stranded when the bus takes off without her.*

TIP *The closer you get to your punch line, the clearer your message must be. Slow down a little. Plant yourself physically because movement distracts. Speak into your microphone. Take pains with your enunciation.*

If after you deliver your punch line, you see people asking their neighbors, "What was that?" you blew it.

8. Remember the Rule of Threes

Whenever possible, group information or points in sets of three. Great literature relies upon the rule of threes, as does comedy. Here are a few popular groupings of three:

- "On land, on the sea, and in the air."
- Father, Son, and Holy Ghost
- Flopsy, Mopsy, and Cottontail
- "Of the people, by the people, and for the people"
- The Nina, the Pinta, the Santa Maria

When the characters in your stories act, have them repeat their acts three times. In comedy, bits are usually funny the third time they happen.

9. Find a Good Slant

Next time you stand in line at the grocery store, look over the magazine rack. Three magazines may feature the same topic, but each will treat the topic differently. So, one will run a headline asking, "Too tired to spend time with your family?" Another will say, "How to have the energy to succeed at work." Yet another will whisper, "Don't let fatigue ruin your sex life." The different approaches to the topic of fatigue represent the writers' slants. Likewise, speakers need to have a slant to their material when we tell our stories.

As Donald Davis says, "When we look at a photograph we see not only the scene captured by the photographer but we also see where the photographer stood to take the picture." That vantage point can enhance our interest.

For example, a story about a teacher who helped you in school could have the following slants:

- appreciation for her dedication
- remembrance of how she made the subject matter come alive
- adult understanding of how she viewed each child as unique and filled with possibilities

When searching for a good slant, mentally walk around your story. See it from all vantage points.

10. End Load Your Material

Within a punch line you'll find a "punch word," a word that when taken by itself seems nondescript but when placed correctly in a story or joke creates the laugh. The best laughs come when the punch word is the last word spoken.

WHERE TO BEGIN YOUR STORY

Novelist Janet Burroway uses her brother as a sounding board for her novels. Once, after spending many months writing, Burroway sent him 10 pages of a book. He sent back the book, slashed through the first 7 pages, and noted, "Your story begins on page 8."

Your storytelling will improve if you too, cut to the important part and then start. The Story Building Chart (see Figure 6.2) can help you get into your story more quickly. You may

Figure 6.2

STORY-BUILDING CHART

Working Title for Story:	
1. Character	
2. Background	
3. Action(s)	
4. Climax	
5. Resolution	
Take-Away or Point:	

need to go through several spare "pages" to get yourself into the mental mindset of the story, but your listener doesn't. Most of us err by waxing eloquent at the wrong time.

Begin your story as close to the action as possible. Not a moment too soon. Not a moment too late. As you review your story, ask yourself again and again, "What could I leave out?" Work backward from the point of the climax. How much of the action does the listener need to hear? Make your story dense by using vibrant verbs, and you will cut your story's length.

PRACTICING YOUR STORY

Now, you've considered all the elements of your story. You've tightened it. You've worked with it. But it isn't really yours until you practice it.

There are six good reasons to practice your story out loud:

1. To Develop Muscle Memory

Human beings have two types of memory: muscle memory and cerebral memory. Muscle memory takes over when you have done a task so often that you no longer engage your brain. For example, pretend for a moment that you are brushing your teeth. You certainly don't rehearse the steps of putting on the toothpaste and positioning the brush in your mouth, do you? In fact, most dentists will tell you that if you changed the way you brush your teeth once in a while, you'd probably do a better job. Your muscles know how to brush your teeth, and therefore, you don't need to think about it. Alternately, cerebral memory involves our brain by requiring that we actually "think" to remember. To deliver a story accurately, you need to develop both muscle memory and cerebral memory.

2. To Make the Story Vocally Appealing

There is a vast difference between writing a story and telling it. Words look one way and sound another. To be able to tell a story without stumbling, you need to be able to wrap your mouth around the words. As you speak the words, you'll hear awkward phrasing. Tape recording your story offers one way to make sure you create a story that sounds good. As you listen to the tape, you'll hear where words might confuse the listener. For example, if you are talking about a learning sequence in training, you might explain that the sequence covers these elements: Know, show, do, critique and reward. That looks pretty straightforward on the printed page. Now, say these words out loud: *know, show, do, critique,* and *reward.* If you listen carefully, you'll immediately hear how this sequence could be misinterpreted, leaving the listener to think you are saying, "No show, do, critique, and reward." The two sets of ideas represent entirely different concepts, yet how is the poor listener to know which you mean?

By listening to your story with an ear for how it sounds, you will note those particularly troublesome homophones, words that sound alike but differ in meaning. You will also note words and phrases that seem awkward or are hard to say. When I wrote speeches for Japanese executives, my boss and I would comb through my scripts for words that were difficult for the Japanese to pronounce and make appropriate changes. Thus, instead of an executive saying, "We will have a little wait before production begins," he would wind up saying, "We will have a short wait before production begins." In this way, we compensated for the difficulty most Japanese have in pronouncing the letter *l.*

3. In the Process of Speaking the Story, You Will Refine and Perfect the Tale

By telling the story out loud, you can find out whether the story works or needs work. Jeff Slutsky, the author of *Streetfighting: Low-Cost Advertising/Promotion Strategies for Your Small Business,* admits that he tries his stories out at NSA conferences and in any general conversation when he can slip in a tale he's perfecting. Grady Jim Robinson takes the process a step further. Robinson notes where the laughs come the first time he tells the story. The second time, he edits out as much as possible that preceded the first laugh. If the laugh falls at a different place the second time, he may even drop the first laugh and start the story at the point where he knows he'll get a good solid laugh most of the time. With each telling, Robinson will refine where the laughs come and edit out the excess.

4. You Give Yourself the Chance to Practice What You Will Do If You Tell the Story Wrong

Jeanne Robertson, author of *Mayberry Humor across the USA,* practices her stories while walking the beaches of North Carolina. If she misspeaks as she tells the story, she practices how she will recover from her mistake. The old rule that practice makes perfect is not nearly as useful as the new rule that realistic practice makes perfect. We are imperfect creatures. By handling imperfection in our practice sessions, we can sail over bumps in the road without winding up in the ditch.

5. You Keep the Story Accessible within Your Memory

If you don't practice your stories on a regular basis, they won't be there for you when you need them. Ah, those rascally stories are as fickle as a honeybee in a field of pink clover. They flit in and out of our minds, leaving us with tantalizing half memories. You can't tell a half story and get results. You have to keep claiming ownership of your stories by practicing them.

6. Practicing Stories Helps Them Grow

Lucky you if all your stories develop and rise like bread made with active yeast. More likely, you too will be the proud owner of stories that just, sorta, kinda fall flat. You know they could be wonderful, but they aren't there yet. What to do? Keep telling that half-baked story. Either you will find a way to create a piece that works or the Universe will step in and take pity on you and send you a gift—a listener who can help you put the finishing touch on your story.

For instance, I once had a story about a raccoon's tail that simply refused to live up to my expectations. Then, I shared it over breakfast with Sharon Bowman and her friend Ross Barnett.

> My son Michael and I were out walking when we spotted a dead raccoon by the side of the road. Having seen *Davy Crockett* a few weeks before, Michael decided that he had to have the raccoon's tail to wear like Fess Parker did in the movie. After much deliberation—and a lot of begging and pleading on Michael's part—I agreed to come back the next day with a knife and cut off the tail. I reasoned this was a cheap way to help my son live out his fantasies.

When my husband got home that night and saw the raccoon tail in the laundry sink, he freaked out. "We could all die of disease!" he shouted. After calming him down, I agreed to call our veterinarian and ask if we were endangered by the raccoon's tail. The vet told me there was a possibility that the raccoon had had rabies, and he strongly urged me to get rid of the tail and the knife and to scour our sink with bleach. First, I had to promise Michael that I'd replace the real tail with a $25 fake "coonskin" cap. Then I threw out my $18 knife and the tail. Finally, I rinsed the sink with boiling water and bleach which ate through the skin on my hands and caused me to have to buy a $12 bottle of heavy duty hand lotion. The total cost of my raccoon tail escapade came to about $55.

At this point in the story, Ross looked at me sagely and said, "And, Joanna, here is the moral to your story: There's no such thing as a free piece of tail."

SEVEN LEVELS OF PRACTICING YOUR STORIES

The little boy walked solemnly to the center of the stage. With great presence, he pulled his violin from its case and tucked it under his chin. Then, with a faraway look in his eyes, he began to play "Twinkle, Twinkle Little Star." The sound was excruciating. He missed notes and screeched as he slid from one note to another up and down the instrument. Parents struggled not to laugh. All across the auditorium, people shifted nervously in their seats. A few consciously rearranged their faces to indicate perfect acceptance. After the assembly, one mother sought out the mother of the violinist. "Oh, I'm sure the crowd must have made him very nervous," sputtered the consoling parent. The violinist's mother looked surprised and said, "I don't think so. That's exactly the way he's been practicing it at home."

Practicing may seem strange to the beginning speaker, but speaker greats like Mark Sanborn put hours and hours of energy into practice. There are many levels of practice.

1. Mental Rehearsal

At this level, you look at the material and go over it in your mind. This level is most useful for material you know or give often. WARNING: Often, when we have given a presentation recently or to a similar group, we tell ourselves, "I know this stuff cold," only to find that we don't. We approach the materials with our minds on cruise control, and when we stand up in front of the group, we discover that the material is much more illusive than we had imagined. A little fear is a healthy signal that we value our audiences and are committed to our best performances no matter how often we've presented this same material.

The best time for mental rehearsal is before you fall asleep the night before the presentation and when you first wake up. These twilight times yield fertile results because your mind shifts from one state of consciousness to another, providing a portal into your memory. To further aid your memory, consider using a tape designed to improve retention, such as *Remembrance,* by Hemi-Sync.

2. Mumble, Mumble Rehearsal

Here you mouth the words and go through your outline to get sequencing down, but you don't "get into" the material. Basically, your goal is to promote muscle memory and to jog your cerebral memory.

Mumble, mumble rehearsing works well on airplanes and other places where you don't want to be too obvious. The drawback is that mumble, mumble does not engage your emotions and only superficially involves your brain.

3. Tape Review

When I was working as a corporate speechwriter for Diamond-Star Motors, the executives shared a problem with me. Because their time was so tightly scheduled, they had little opportunity to practice their speeches. However, a quick investigation revealed a wasted pocket of time they could use: drive time. Since Diamond-Star was a joint venture between Mitsubishi and Chrysler, many executives regularly drove to Detroit for meetings. By taping the speech for them—including the inflections and pauses—we allowed them to pop in a tape and review the speech in the car.

Any parent can tell you that when you play Barney or Raffi on the daily drive to daycare, your child can soon repeat ad nauseam and verbatim every tune on the tape. What's even more pitiful is when the poor parent walks into a high-powered meeting humming, "I love you, you love me . . . ." and realizes the tune has insidiously lodged itself in the dark recesses of the adult brain.

The down side of the tape review is that you don't engage the larger use of the brain because you are relying on rote memory. The up side is how painless this is. In addition, making the tape offers you a great way to time your material, as long as you realize that tape-time and real-time-with-audience can vary. By keeping a library of tapes of your presentations and using your outlines so that you have the "perfect" stuff, you can keep yourself up to speed on a variety of presentations with minimal effort. You can also create a tape solely of your stories, told independently of presentations. This catalogs them and keeps them accessible.

4. Tape and Trigger Review

This variation on the tape review theme involves a tad more effort on your part but provides terrific results. You can do it one of three ways:

■ Tape your presentation and simply turn off the tape at key points to practice stories or segues.

■ Tape your presentation in outline form, leaving empty spaces which you then fill in with your story or segue.

■ Tape your presentation in outline and say, "Turn off the tape and do the XYZ story."

Each method allows you to practice the portions of a presentation that are most likely to be difficult, yet they each keep you on track and remind you of sequence.

TIP *Speakers often fall into two categories: locked-in sequencers and flexible sequencers. Consider which you are when you choose audio-visual materials, because they can lock you into giving a presentation that is linear.*

When you use slides, you have no latitude about sequencing. You can't stop a presentation and rearrange the slides, although many speakers will flip through the slides to go backward or forward as need be. For locked-in sequencers, a change in the sequence can be difficult or impossible. Computer-generated presentations also lock the presenter into a sequence. Although the computer-generated programs do offer the chance to change your presentation seconds before you go on, once you are on, the sequence in the computer must be handled in a linear fashion.

Conversely, overheads—old-fashioned and bulky as they are—offer more flexibility. You can skip one and set it aside without the audience ever knowing.

Why might you need to make a last minute change? Listen to one presenter's story and imagine how you might handle the situation:

> I was giving a presentation on business writing. To illustrate the problem of misplaced modifiers, I had an overhead with this joke: Straight Man—I know a man with a wooden leg named Smith. Funny Man—What's the name of his other leg? As I was arranging my materials, the education coordinator walked in. She had an artificial limb! I excused myself and pulled the overhead quickly and stuffed it into the bottom of my briefcase.

Imagine how much more stress she might have felt trying to pull the correct slide from the carousel or to delete the overhead from the computer!

Presenters often rely on slides and overheads as story triggers. Instead of memorizing a sequence of points, they know that by putting up one slide or overhead after another, they'll stay on track.

5. Informal Rehearsal

In this situation, you actually give your presentation, but you don't worry about the setting. Informal rehearsal can take place in the shower (laminate your notes, please!), while walking your dog, and in front of a mirror. Any place you want to rehearse will work, as long as distractions and interruptions are held to a minimum.

The up side of the informal rehearsal rests with its versatility. By talking your way through your shower, walking the dog, and folding laundry, you can squeeze a lot of practice into your daily life. The down side happens when we don't get the chance to use our equipment or study our gestures. (So far, I have not used folding towels as a gesture on the platform . . . but who knows?) A few experts have suggested that creativity

manifests full-force in the shower. I agree, but if you are planning a full day of training, you might run out of hot water.

The informal rehearsal integrates ongoing practice with
good time-management skills. A few hearty souls, like Patricia
Fripp, even carry notepads with them as they walk so that
they can take notes as they practice.

6. Dress Rehearsal

If you've ever been in a play, you know all about dress
rehearsals. They are as much like the real performance as possible, incorporating all elements of dress, equipment, and site.
Particularly for beginning speakers, dress rehearsals should be
incorporated into the practice schedule. By dressing the way
you plan to dress, you double-check how your chosen outfit
looks and, most important, where the microphone will go.
For women, this presents a challenge. If you are wearing a
one piece dress, the battery pack of the clip-on microphone
must fit in a pocket of the dress if you have no waistband. If
you are wearing a jewel or scoop neckline without a fold of
material around the throat, it may be difficult to clip on a
microphone.

You can solve these problems by wearing a suit and a
blouse that buttons up to the neck. (Wearing the microphone
on the lapel doesn't always work. The microphone may or
may not pick up your voice at that distance.) Or you can use
a hand-held microphone or a lavaliere microphone, which
hangs around the neck like a necklace.

Men wearing suits with ties have the perfect locations to
clip on a microphone (the tie or lapel) and to wear the battery pack (the waistband of your slacks).

Of course, dress rehearsals also offer other advantages.
You can practice using your audio-visual materials. You can
practice using the entire physical space where you are pre-

senting. (After watching a keynote, NSA's first president and speech coach Bill Gove lamented that many speakers scrunch themselves into a corner, ignoring the expanse of stage open to them. Consider the room you have for your presentation and how you will use it to best advantage.) You can check to make sure your audio-visual materials show up from all vantage points.

During a dress rehearsal—whether on site or not—you should practice your gestures and timing as if you had an audience. Use a clock or a beeper that vibrates at intervals to let you know how much time you are using.

TIP *Now, having told you of the importance of dress rehearsals, I must be honest and admit that you'll probably have too few chances to do a full-blown dress rehearsal in your career. Often, the first time you see your venue is shortly before the meeting. Whenever possible, try to arrive in advance and at least test your microphone and audio-visual materials. Professionals such as Michael McKinley, former president of the NSA, even bring duct tape and a screw-in spotlight. McKinley will work with the on-site staff to get more light on the spot where he will be standing. Strangely enough, how well people hear us has more to do with how well they can see us than with how high the volume is. McKinley knows this and uses the spotlight to be as visible as possible. And the duct tape? McKinley tapes doors so the latch mechanism won't snap as people enter and leave his presentation. He creates bright-colored signs to tape on the doors that say, "Quiet please! Presentation in progress!" Many speakers rely on masking tape to block off back rows, forcing the crowd to sit up front and tightly packed. This density builds energy in the room.*

As speakers, we cannot control every aspect of our presentation, but we are responsible for controlling as much of the venue as we can.

7. Lights, Camera, Action

The last way to rehearse involves using a video camera. By delivering your presentation on tape, you can see yourself the way your audience sees you. Nothing works as well for pointing out nervous gestures and irritating habits we all have. If possible, you should not only tape your practice but also regularly have yourself taped as you give your presentation.

Like most of us, you'll die a thousand deaths. You'll hear every disfluency. Note every stutter. And commit to lose weight. But . . . the upside is how much you will learn. There is no substitute for video, painful as it is. Your presentation skills will soar as you review and learn from your mistakes.

TIP *Speaker Nancy Nix-Rice, author of* Looking Good: A Comprehensive Guide to Wardrobe Planning, Color & Personal Style Development, *has these suggestions on how to dress for video:*

- The camera's eye is far less forgiving than the eyes of your audience, so pay attention to visible details when you are being filmed. Simple, tailored styles show up better than fussy ones. High-contrast color combinations convey the greatest authority, but contrast is magnified on video. Consider wearing pale blue with navy or charcoal grey instead of stark black and white.
- Colors from the teal-turquoise-jade family send a friendly message and are universally flattering. Women can use these colors well for blouses or jackets, and they make good necktie choices for male speakers.
- Avoid bright red; it "bleeds" on film, making any area it covers appear fuzzy and somewhat enlarged.
- Watch out for plaids or geometric prints, which can appear to come alive on film, wiggling wildly and distracting viewers.

- ▪ Accessories complete the picture. Earrings should be large enough to add presence to your look—at least the size of a nickel, no larger than a quarter. Skip any shiny metal that might glare under bright lighting.
- ▪ A necktie hanging askew can ruin an otherwise polished look. Tie bars are passé, but double-stick tape is an invisible solution.
- ▪ Double-check your hairstyle from every angle, then hold it in place with your favorite styling product.

GET BY WITH A LITTLE HELP FROM YOUR FRIENDS: A LABORATORY APPROACH TO PRACTICE

Not ready for prime time? A group of speakers near Chicago decided to meet together on a regular basis to critique each other's materials, to work on stories, and to discuss a variety of aspects of the speaking business. They call themselves the Lab Rats™, and their names are M. J. Cross, Nadine Grant, Pamela Meyer, and Mari Pat Varga, the author of *Great Openings and Closing: Launch and Land Your Presentations with Punch, Power, and Pizazz.*

Lab Rats™ began when four speaker friends came together in an effort to share what they were learning and to have a place to explore new ideas. According to Varga, the name reflected their desire to "foster a laboratory-like setting where we could experiment."

You, too, can form a similar mastermind group. Link up with other speakers whose judgments you trust.

TIP *Five essentials have kept the Lab Rats™ working together successfully for more than three years:*

1. **A mission statement.** They began with a mission statement to dissect and perfect their keynoting skills and content.

2. **A meeting format.** Meeting bimonthly, they begin with a half hour devoted to catching up. Then, using a timer, they each get exactly one half hour to work on the material of their own choosing.

3. **A decision about how you will work together.** According to Varga, "a typical segment might involve working in a new vignette or anecdote. We begin that process by providing copies of the story for all to review. A lively and thoughtful exchange follows the reading—editorial suggestions may be proposed, the story's focus examined, or new angles and direction recommended. Such an anecdote may appear meeting after meeting as the speaker fine-tunes its contents and eventually 'performs' the piece."

4. **Bring in an outsider.** Because their friendships have evolved with their meetings, the Lab Rats™ admit it is hard to remain objective. Therefore, they occasionally bring in an outsider to add a new point of view. Once they invited a classical storyteller; another time it was a professional acting coach.

5. **Reevaluate the group's direction.** Occasionally, they check to make sure they are meeting the needs of the members. You may even decide the time has come to disband or add a new person.

Varga sums it up nicely: "Do these five steps always produce a dynamic learning experience with other professional speakers? No. Chemistry, mutual respect, trust, and commitment are also essential ingredients for a successful group."

A TOAST
TO TOASTMASTERS

Although many people think of Toastmasters International as an organization for folks who want to overcome their fear of professional speaking, it really goes beyond that by offering a terrific opportunity to learn and practice all sorts of presentations. So, even if stagefright isn't your problem, you may wish to join a local chapter as a great place to practice your work.

Because Toastmasters' meetings are set up to give members the chance to practice speaking, they offer a great place to try your stories. Usually, one person evaluates another in a formal procedure. However, if you are practicing a story, try to get as much input and feedback as possible. Pass out index cards and ask that everyone in the group share comments. Although they may not be able to talk with you during the course of the meeting, they can pass in the cards or chat with you at a break.

The sequence of speeches to be given in Toastmasters is structured, and you may wish to practice a story that doesn't fit the next speech you are scheduled to give. You may wish to discuss this with your Toastmasters' president and see how to work around this problem.

SUMMARY

In this chapter, we looked more closely at the key elements of a story. The speaker can shape many elements, including voice, persona, pace, repetitive theme or golden thread, circular construction, and audience participation to increase the dramatic potential of the story. By remembering the essentials of crafting a story, you can improve the impact your story has on the audience. The story-building chart in this chapter helps you break down the elements within your story so you can better fine-tune them. Finally, we have illustrated the levels at which you can practice your story.

EXERCISES

1. Choose a story to examine more closely. Note the various parts of the story: the build-up with character devel-

opment and foreshadowing, if any; the action or building conflict; the punch line, punch word, or trigger word; and the dénouement.

2. Using another story or a book as a model, describe how the character was developed. Look for concrete information about the character as well as more subtle information.

3. Watch a video of a professional speaker who is a dynamic storyteller. Choose a story to study. In what voice was the story told? What was the speaker's persona? How did the speaker alter his or her pace before, during, and after the story?

4. Graph an entire presentation by a professional speaker. Compare graphs with others in your class, having everyone graph a different speaker. Which graph shows the most variety? Watch that speaker's tape as a class. How does the variety impact the speaker's overall presentation?

5. Watch for a repetitive theme or golden thread in your speaker's presentation. If someone in the class finds a repetitive theme or golden thread, have him or her share the presentation with the class. Can the class find the repetitive theme or golden thread?

6. Watch for a speech with circular construction. If someone in your class finds a speech made in a circular construction, ask him or her to share it with the class.

7. Look for examples of audience participation in the presentations you view. List the stages of participation you notice.

8. Choose a personal story and begin to work on it. Review the essentials of crafting a terrific story. Record the story before you begin to work on it and after.

9. Chart your story on the story-building chart.

10. Practice your story at the differing levels suggested in this chapter.

7 Using Stories Wisely

I was part of the middle class and stayed there until my family blew apart at the seams when I was eight. My parents divorced, and the three kids were split off to different relatives. We never did reassemble as a family. I ended up practically on welfare and remember a Christmas dinner of corn flakes and warm powdered milk. There were no presents or tree. I have told this story to fewer than six people in my life because it evokes a sympathy which is now beside the point. I relate it here because it illustrates the problem most of us have had: at some point in our lives, we have suffered indignities caused by lack of money.

Paul Hawken, *Growing a Business*

Of all the men in the Liars' Club, Daddy told the best stories. . . . No matter how many tangents he took or how far the tale flew from its starting point before he reeled it back, he had this gift: he knew how to be believed.

Mary Karr, *The Liars' Club*

HOW TO TELL WHEN AND WHEN NOT TO USE A STORY

You've worked on it. You love it. You want to tell it. But should you? Maybe your story isn't right for this audience, this presentation, or for you.

Grady Jim Robinson says, "Understanding the context of an event and the audience may be the most underrated talent of a consistently successful humorist and speaker." *Relationship speaking,* a term coined by Robinson, calls for the speaker to build a contextual bridge between the platform and the audience. Aspects of the context to consider include the following:

1. **What happens/happened immediately before the speaker's presentation?** One speaker was appalled by what he heard as he stood in the wings ready to go on. The president of the company that had hired him was announcing massive layoffs. And the president concluded his remarks with, "You have only yourselves to blame. Here's the motivational speaker."

2. **Who is the audience?** Trying to inject a little humor into a presentation, a speaker made a joke about how former vice president Dan Quayle was doomed to always play second fiddle. Only after watching the faces of the audience fall and struggling through the next hour of her presentation did she learn that Huntington, Indiana, the place where she was speaking, was Quayle's hometown. The more you know about your audience, the better you can match their needs by telling the right story.

3. **Who is the speaker?** A double standard exists concerning offensive language. Audiences expect women speakers to adhere to a much higher standard of conduct than men. Using foul language is never a smart idea, and for women it can be deadly.

4. **What is the purpose of the gathering?** If this is a mandatory meeting, the group will be more serious than if this is an annual conference with an award banquet. In the mandatory meeting situation, the speaker must overcome the audience's initial reticence. At the banquet, the speaker must acknowledge the celebratory nature of the gathering.

5. **What is the overall mood of the group?** Of course, this goes hand-in-hand with the group's purpose. A dinner banquet with free-flowing liquor has ruined the presentation of many a speaker. If a group is in the mood to get wild and crazy, a serious presentation will not be well received.

Misreading any of these signals can be disastrous. Robinson notes that the ability to size up the audience and know what it needs is almost intuitive. Van Cliburn says that as he plays a concert, a part of him always stays with the audience, viewing the performance from the vantage point of his listeners. Speakers, too, must always keep a peripheral sense of what is going on with the audience as they present.

Most speakers develop an intuitive feel for audiences over time. There is no substitute in the speaking business for speaking. When confronted by the myriad of different possible situations and the unique challenges of each presentation, the speaker must rise to the imperfect occasion. Each time you present, you learn a little more about speaking, about audiences, and about yourself. Your goal should be to develop consistency. Ed Hearn, a former professional baseball player, says, "As a ballplayer, that's what being a pro is all about: consistency. As a professional speaker, that's what I deliver as well."

WHEN YOU SHOULD AVOID USING THE STORY

Great as a story may sound, there are times when you shouldn't tell it.

1. When the Story Isn't Yours

The speaker who is limited to rehashing anecdotes about famous people or telling stories gleaned from other sources is playing a risky game. True, an insightful story about Churchill may be the perfect way to drive home your point about determination. But talking about Churchill may actually be more risky than talking about the time you were called upon to show great tenacity in your own life.

Here's why: You invite instant comparison to any other speaker who also might use this story. The worst-case example of this occurs when two speakers on the same program tell the exact same story. It happens all the time. In fact, at one conference the same story popped up not once, not twice, but *three* times. Imagine how the audience reacted! Meeting planners hate situations like this because when they buy you, they are buying *your original material.* Rehashed stories make the meeting planner and the audience wonder what else in your presentation is not yours.

Remember: **It is unethical to use another speaker's story and tell it as your own.** You will never, ever be accepted as a professional if you do.

Perhaps you are reading this and thinking, "What's the big deal? How can a person own a story? How can it hurt a speaker if I borrow a story or a joke while I'm getting started?" It does hurt. Look again and you'll see why:

1. **It hurts the speaker who developed the story.** Jeanne Robertson's famous baton story has been stolen and retold by so many other people that Robertson has lost jobs because meeting planners say, "Oh, we had a speaker tell that story last year." Is that fair to Robertson? No. Theft is theft. And when you steal, you become a thief.

2. **It hurts the audience.** Robertson's story will never be told as well by you as it is by her. You try to tell it and you cheat all your listeners out of the experience of knowing Robertson firsthand.

3. **It hurts the meeting planner.** The planner hired you in good faith and you returned that good faith by passing off counterfeit material.

4. **It hurts the speaking industry.** More and more, we hear planners and bureaus saying, "You speakers all sound alike." Of course we do if we steal each other's material.

5. **You hurt yourself.** You could have been sharing from your life. You could have been growing as a professional and developing your own material. Instead, you tried to take a shortcut on the career path and cheated yourself

out of honoring your uniqueness. You will have a harder time marketing yourself because the best you can be is an imitation, a cheapened copy of the real storyteller. A few other ways that you hurt yourself:

■ You may bore your listeners because they may already know the story. Unless they are unusually polite, at least one or two people may whisper the punch line to the person sitting beside them.

■ You have dramatically increased your chances of forgetting what you intended to say. After all, you had to memorize this material in order to present it. Chances are it's only stored in your short-term memory, a place notorious for its poor filing system.

■ Your gestures will probably look wooden and planned. Remember, it's not your story. You can't rely on your recall of your emotions to help you recreate the story. Instead you are forced to act out this story, which is much more difficult than recalling feelings.

■ You can't do the story justice. A copy of a copy is called a second-generation copy, and the second generation is never as clear or sharp as the original. Your "borrowed" story won't be, either.

■ You have lost the opportunity to build a meaningful relationship with the people who are there to hear *you!*

TIP *Professional speakers often talk about "signature stories," stories that are original with that speaker and become that speaker's story trademark. Signature stories vary widely in content: Michael Scott Karpovich is known for his "swirly" story; W Mitchell for the story of his life; Jeanne Robertson for her baton story; Liz Curtis Higgs for problems with her pantyhose; Grady Jim Robinson for his white satin basketball shorts and pine tar story; Patricia Fripp for "Froggy" and personal responsibility; and Jeff Slutsky for chartering a Lear Jet to get to a speaking engagement.*

Beginning speakers with discriminating palates often steal from the best. In this case, imitation is not flattering but problematic. When Mark Mayfield unknowingly followed another speaker who told Mayfield's trademark story about a crashing head table, Mayfield lost his credibility. What did he do next? Mayfield confronted the offender, gently, and suggested that both of them looked bad because of the theft.

Mayfield points out that you can't steal an idea or a concept; theft really occurs in the details. Therefore, two speakers could tell stories about their spouses' hatred for their pet cats, and each could be highly original. The problem would occur if both speakers claimed that their spouses said, "It's me or the cat," and the speaker responded, "If you change your mind . . . "

Develop your own signature story. Look through your life for those situations that really made a difference. Ask yourself, "What was a turning point for me?" From those will come what James C. Humes has called "soul shakers." Humes points out that they all "touch on such emotionally charged subjects as God, country, family, or death." Embarrassing moments would also rise to the top of the list, along with the challenges of growing up. These key experiences underscore the "most personal is most universal" rule. Look at your life, share authentically, and you will always make an impact.

You were given your life for a purpose. Use your unique experiences to develop a voice that is truly one-of-a-kind. As Rosita Perez, author of *The Music Is You*, explains,

Many speakers are content with sharing their skills and educating. When we realize, however, that there is much more to it than that, we find creative ways of putting it out there. I am not saying it is easy. Or even without risk. The joy will come in realizing you are really making a difference, instead of a speech.

2. When the Story Might Be Slanderous

Libel occurs when a falsehood is written; slander occurs when a falsehood is spoken. Even if the story is true, you might hesitate to tell it. Hiding the identity of the person involved in a negative story safeguards you and the meeting planner. The exception would be when the story has appeared in publication and you are merely retelling what is common knowledge. Of course, you are also free to share a negative situation that happened to you personally. So, if you talk about customer service, you can tell about the time XYZ company wouldn't give you a refund—as long as you are accurate and honest in what you say.

"Talking trash" and slinging mud leave both you and your object with dirt on your hands. Before you tell a tale of woe, think it through carefully. Make sure the story doesn't reflect poorly on you.

3. When the Story Is a Chestnut

A woman got up at a conference, walked to the podium, and announced, "The officers of our association have asked me to read my little poem. They do enjoy it so." The keynote speaker was stunned to hear the exact poem another speaker uses at the conclusion of each of his presentations. The crowd loved the poem and applauded heartily for the "author." She smiled as she sat down and handed the keynoter a copy of the poem. "Folks, love this. You might want to use it, too, " she had written generously in the margin.

Not a chance. First of all, the name of the person who wrote the poem has long disappeared, so giving credit where credit is due would be difficult, if not impossible. And second, at the rate that particular poem is making the circuit, everyone will have heard it. Third, what if two speakers with the same poem get asked to speak to the same crowd? The poem has lost its value because it has now become a chestnut, an overused piece of uncertain origin.

Have you ever tasted cold, stale chestnuts? Don't bother. They're awful. Overused and stale, that's the chestnut—a story that has been told too many times by too many people. Avoid them at all costs. They are the clichés of the speaking business.

4. When the Story Is Therapeutic for You but Has Not Been Mythologized

In the quest to become authentic, a few speakers have used the platform to share the deepest, darkest, unprocessed secrets of their lives. Bad idea. It's speaking, folks, not therapy. You don't have the right to drag the audience through your stuff because you hurt.

Quick—what's the difference between raw sewage and methane? Processing. Take that painful episode in your life and mythologize it. Process the situation and find the growth potential inside, and then share your lesson if it is appropriate for this presentation.

What are the signs that your story needs more time and distance? Do you cry every time you tell it? BZZT. Wrong. Does your audience get so upset that they can't move on, they get stuck emotionally in your story? BZZT. Wrong. Are you only 90 percent comfortable with what you just shared? BZZT. Wrong.

Mari Pat Varga, a speaker and trainer, uses the 90 percent rule as a guide: "If I'm only 90 percent comfortable, then I know my audience will pick up on that 10 percent unsureness. And that means I'm taking too big of a risk." Trust your gut. If you are concerned, hold back, rethink, and repackage it.

5. When the Story Is Wrong for the Audience

A predominantly male, all-business audience may not respond well to a cute story about your kid, even if it perfectly illustrates a point you want to make. Nor, typically, will women in the audience appreciate lots of sports terms and inside jokes about different football teams. Be sensitive to the differences in topics preferred by each gender. For example, the president of a large company once lost half his audience because he switched midspeech from being the leader of the organization to sounding like a guy at a sports bar who was goofing around with his buddies.

In the same manner, telling your audience about problems you've had getting your BMW serviced will not play well if the median income of the group is less than $30,000. True, this may sound like stereotypical thinking. But, in this case, we are discussing matters of common sense. The name of the game in speaking is inclusion, not exclusion. When you pick a topic that doesn't connect with your audience and where they are at that given moment, they exclude you.

Think through the composition of the audience—and its purpose. If members are gathered for a hard-hitting business conference, your cute family story may stick out like a person in a clown suit. You have to take people from where they are to where you want them to go. Starting with a business story or a story about their industry will tell them that you understand how seriously they take themselves. Once the ice melts, you can share a story of a more personal nature.

TIP *The rule seems to be that the more left-brain the occupation, the more number-, fact-, and business-oriented your stories must be. Left-brain occupations include accounting, engineering, research and development, and science. The more right-brain the group, the more humor and personal anecdotes you can use safely.*

You can make your stories more left-brain by including a number, for instance, "Researchers tell us that 45 percent of all household chores are done by men," and then using a story for support. You can also make your information more left-brain by numbering it: "Let me tell you the three secrets of success . . . ."

6. When the Story Is Wrong for You

In her book *Enter Talking,* Joan Rivers says that when she was a beginning comic, her mentors and agents created personas for her that did not match her personality. But Rivers believed in herself and her comic abilities. When she adopted the persona of the single, Jewish girl whose parents longed for her to marry, Rivers found herself and her career skyrocketed.

Who are you? Who does the audience think you are? If your message doesn't match who they perceive you to be, you will fail. Without congruity, your message doesn't ring true. Your verbal and nonverbal messages must match exactly. When conflict occurs between verbal and nonverbal messages, nonverbal always wins. The body rarely lies, and most of us can't fake the message we send unconsciously. If we could, more people would win Oscars.

7. When the Story Might Offend Anyone In or Out of the Room

George stepped confidently to the podium and spoke in beautiful dulcet tones: "Statistics are interesting things. They give us information, yes, but not always the information we need. For example, in the local paper yesterday, they printed a statistic that 35 percent of the women in this city will commit adultery." He paused, and adjusted his glasses, putting the newspaper clipping in his pocket. "That's interesting but not helpful. What I really want to know is their names and phone numbers."

Now George speaks frequently and enjoys a respectable career as a business consultant. But on this particular occasion, George must have suffered a brain glitch. The audience of 23 meeting planners gave a collective gasp. Two of the four men in the room laughed, nervously. The 19 women sat silent.

You might excuse George by saying that he is a very sweet man. But sweet people don't tell offensive stories. And he did.

TIP *Wondering if your comments will be offensive? Try this two-step test: (1) Insert another word for the name of the group you might offend. Example: Where George said* women *insert* Jews, African Americans, people with handicaps, *etc." Now does it look offensive? This switch helps because we all seem to have blinders that make us more sensitive about one group than about another. (2) Ask several friends who are members of that ethnic, racial, gender, or special needs group if your comments might offend. Ask them to be brutally honest and thank them for their input.*

8. When the Story Invades the Privacy of Another

A woman speaker told a funny story about her husband's difficulty finding a job. Her husband was in the audience. He was not amused. Later she asked, "Do you mind? It always gets a great laugh!" He growled, "Sure it does, at my expense." The cost of the story was high: She sold her husband's goodwill for a few lousy laughs.

Before you share the foibles of your loved ones, clear the story with them. That's the least they deserve. (You might also check with your friends if you use them as examples in a story. They may feel thrilled or they may feel used, and it's better to find out the easy way.)

BREAKING THE RULES

Now that you've learned the rules, you have permission to break them—with caution!

1. You Can Use Another Speaker's Story or Information with Permission

Go to that speaker and ask. If the story is not a signature story, or if the information is common knowledge in another industry, the speaker might give permission. One beginning speaker called a seasoned speaker who had written several books and asked for permission to use the exercises outlined in his books. He told her, "So many people use my stuff and never ask! I'm so delighted by your honesty that I'm giving you the go-ahead. But please reference me on your handouts." She did.

2. If the Story Is Slanderous, Simply Leave Out the Name of the Offender

Instead say, "The president of a major company who shall remain nameless—" and pause.

3. Be Honest with the Group about the Chestnut

"Many of you have probably heard this story, so please bear with me, but I sincerely think this illustrates my point exactly," is one way to introduce a chestnut and retain your audience's goodwill. Lilly Walters suggests that you can also tell a chestnut in a novel way by focusing on a new interpretation. Dewitt Jones retold the worn-out story of a boy tossing starfish back into the ocean by asking, "What if the starfish didn't want to go back into the ocean? What if he spent his whole life trying to make it to that shore?" The unexpected twist brought gales of laughter from his audience.

4. Tell the Story to Your Best Friend or Therapist

If you can't get through it, and you haven't processed it, maybe this is nature's way of saying, "You need help." When you find yourself tempted to abuse the platform, ask, "Am I taking care of myself?" Speaking takes tremendous physical and psychological energy. To be good, you must be totally available and in the moment. You can't do that if you are upset about an occurrence in your personal life. For the sake of your career as a speaker, work through your dramas so they don't travel with you to the platform.

Whenever you find yourself burning with desire to tell the audience about something that just happened to you, beware. This is a good sign that you are acting out of the emotional heat of the moment and not from an awareness of what's best for the presentation.

5. The Story May Not Be Wrong for the Audience If Properly Placed within the Total Presentation

Consider the story's placement in the context of the total presentation before you decide whether or not you can use it. Typically, the more personal a story is, the later you should schedule it in the presentation.

6. Is the Story Wrong for You?

Perhaps you need to change the audience's perception of who you are. When speaking to rural audiences, I purposefully share stories about my rural upbringing. If I didn't, they might doubt that I am being honest when I tell them I used to be flummoxed by escalators. Consider challenging the audience's perception of who you are by sharing the appropriate information they need to change their minds.

7. Sorry. If It Is Offensive, It Is Offensive, and That Can't Be Fixed

The late comedian Denis Wolfberg used to do an entire segment in his act about how he had offended people. Wolfberg would say, "So this woman called and she said how dare you say XYZ!" By putting his words in the mouth of another person, they didn't seem quite so offensive. Wolfberg was a genius. He made comedy out of offensive material, and crowds loved him for it. But Wolfberg was a once-in-a-century comic genius.

One speaker shares a story about being a room father for his children's school. He tells about an unruly child who wrote a naughty word for human waste that begins with *t* and rhymes with *word*. Then the speaker empathizes with the audience, saying, "I know you are as shocked as I was." The speaker sets the story up so that the listener fills in the word, and he never sullies his lips saying the *t* word! By adding his personal reaction, he sides with his audience. He has found a masterful way to share questionable material without offending.

8. You Don't Have to Invade People's Privacy

Simply change the names to protect the innocent. If people have a problem with your sharing a story about them, completely disguise their identities and use the story. You may even go so far as to say, "Here's a story that was told to me," to disguise your involvement with the people in the story. A few phrases that work well are: "A friend of mine told me this story . . . " and "I heard about a person who . . . "

You can further disguise the people in the story by changing their occupations, giving fictitious physical descriptions, or changing where they live. One method that works particularly well is to combine several people into one. Authors frequently do this when creating characters in a book.

IT HURTS SO GOOD

Should you avoid telling a story because it makes people uncomfortable? That depends. Some stories we need to hear if we are going to grow. You may be hired to tell people unpleasant truths. How do you deliver unpleasant information? One way is to let your audience discover it for themselves.

Once, a speaker was hired to work with a government agency that was being downsized. This agency was full of people who had been on board for years. They were furious. Interviews with the agency alerted the speaker to the people's blind spot. Somehow, somewhere, they had convinced themselves that this downsizing was unique to them. They felt they were being treated unfairly.

What could the speaker do? The speaker interviewed employees. Then he went out and researched change. Then, early on in his presentation, he gave the audience a quiz about change, with questions such as, "How many people change jobs each day?" Most people love to test their knowledge, and this group was no different. They eagerly filled out the quiz. As they heard the answers to the questions, they realized that change was happening all around them. Suddenly, it no longer seemed that they were being picked on.

The speaker then followed up the quiz by asking a long-time member of the agency about the changes he had seen in his career. "Well," began the experienced employee, "I sure can think of a big change I've seen. Thirty years ago when we first started having meetings like this, I couldn't attend 'cause they didn't allow coloreds into this hotel."

Silence reigned. The story needed to be told. And, the speaker found a way to tell them without alienating them. True, a few people felt uncomfortable, but the discomfort they felt was growing pains. Don't shy away from stories that cause discomfort. Do use them with care and think about when, where, and how to share them.

TRUTH VERSUS FICTION

This might be the perfect time to have a little discussion about the nature of truth and fiction in storytelling. Because of his own storytelling prowess and because his wife Jonellen is the author of three books of fiction, Lou Heckler explains with a laugh, "The line between truth and fiction in our home gets pretty blurred."

Often, beginning speakers worry too much about telling a story truthfully and too little about telling a story well. We don't need to know every stinky detail. Significant detail sets up the story, and we need detail to make the story come alive, but don't drown your audience in the petty facts of your life.

How truthful do your stories need to be? First of all, they must have a ring of truth. Somehow, someway, they must seem true, or they won't pass your listeners' skepticism screen. For listeners to enjoy a story, they may have to suspend their skepticism as you tell it. The audience agrees with you to enter a place of semi-make-believe. They are willing to be misled, as long as you don't entirely take advantage of them and make them feel embarrassed.

Second, Barry Mann suggests that your stories must always keep an "emotional truth" about them. "Emotional truth" appeals to our higher level of self, the one that operates independently of fact. When information is "emotionally true," we relate to the feeling content instead of the literal content. This validates your audience's willingness to participate in fantasy. After all, if I'm going to let you fool me, it had better be for a good reason. When an audience recognizes the "emotional truth," it is willing to let details slide.

Third, they must be truthful in a fair way. If you trick the audience for self-serving purposes—say a cheap laugh—they will get angry. If the goal of the story was to tell a larger truth, you can be forgiven for minor trickery.

Your listeners will suspend their rational minds and trip with you down fantasy lane if the journey isn't too far out, the destination is noble, and they won't be made fun of on the trip.

Remember, too, that truth will always be stranger than fiction. If you keep your eyes open and read your local paper, you will find obscure and odd real-life stories you can use from the platform. The August 20, 1996, obituary page of the *St. Louis Post-Dispatch* included this gem about Bertram "Bert" Minkin, professional storyteller and free-lance writer:

> In the winter of 1991, Mr. Minkin lived a real-life scare story. He slipped on the ice in a secluded area of University City, breaking his hip. Although he could hear cars whizzing past, he was alone in the cold and getting colder—"like an oyster on ice in a restaurant," as he later described it.
>
> Finally, more than an hour into his ordeal, two 7-year-old boys came across him. One ran for help while the other stayed to comfort him.

The boys were Cub Scouts, and from his hospital bed, Mr. Minkin told them stories of good deeds through the ages. He later described the boys' good deed by saying, "I could never have constructed a story that is more affirming than this."

As the saying goes, "Truth is stranger than fiction." Look first to the truth, then embellish it to make the deeper truth—the vast colors and shades of the human condition—come to life.

POETIC LICENSE

Poetic license is the creative freedom we grant all artists. So when you remember the essence of a story about your first love in kindergarten, the listener will forgive you when you say she had red hair even though you can't really remember whether her hair color was red, brown, or yellow. The listener forgives you because what we want to hear is your story, and the details are important only because they help us, as listeners, to participate on an emotional level in what you say.

As Barry Mann points out, "I am a creative artist and that makes me different from a reporter. Reporters tell facts; storytellers tell truths." When you finish your story about young love and the preschool set, our minds will search for the emotional truth you shared rather than fixate on the color of a little girl's hair.

I DON'T EXAGGERATE; I JUST REMEMBER BIG

Shoot, what fun is it to tell stories if you aren't going to exaggerate a little? Suppose the speaker tells you she was locked in her hotel room. Big deal. Then she increases the conflict by explaining that a crowd was gathering to hear her. Now she could tell you that there were 40 or 50 people. But what if she tells you that there were 500 CEOs waiting for her in a ballroom? And she could tell you she had an hour before she went on. But what if she told you she had only 15 minutes? And she could tell you she was on the first floor. But what if she told you her room was on the third floor, and she kept looking out the window and wondering, "Do I toss down my shoes first? Or do I wear them to protect my feet when I jump?"

See how with each exaggeration of the situation, the intensity cranks up another notch? A simple story, with its volume turned up to the limit, metamorphoses into a funny and dramatic anecdote when you "remember big."

ASK THE MAGIC QUESTION

Best stories happen when you ask yourself, "What if?" Take that story you "remembered big," and ask, "What if the janitor still didn't come? What could I have done?" Think of the most outlandish solution to your problem.

Think back to when you were a child and your mama said, "Eat all your food. Don't you know there are children starving in Africa?" And your mind filled in the logical solution, "What if we send them our garbage?"

Take any story you are working with, and ask yourself, "What if?" Imagine your poor sainted mother. What would drive her bonkers? Imagine your prim and proper English teacher. What would have caused her to faint? Be creative. Begin with the truth and fantasize the most fantastic situation possible to create a memorable story.

WHEN NOT TO INDULGE IN FANTASY

In days of old, speakers would tell a chestnut and put themselves in the center of the action. Because the stories weren't new or fresh, listeners quickly caught on to the fact that they were being lied to. For example, a man told an audience,

I saw an amazing situation at the airport that reminded me of the power of being polite. A guy—obviously in a hurry—began yelling at a skycap to hurry up and process his luggage. The skycap didn't respond; he simply kept processing the man's luggage. The angry guy began to yell louder at the poor airline employee. The skycap merely smiled and handed the man his baggage claim ticket. I couldn't resist. I had to know the skycap's secret for keeping his cool while a customer mistreated him. "Well," said the skycap, "He was having a bad day. He is flying to Alaska and his suitcases are all going to Jamaica."

This story is older than the Wright brothers. If all the speakers who have ever told it really were at the airport at the same time, it could only have been an NSA convention.

Each time a speaker uses an old chestnut and thinks he or she is "customizing" it by saying, "It happened to me," he or she is really playing poor odds that the audience will know better. At the least, a few people will roll their eyes. At the worst, a raconteur will repeat the punch line, causing an entire row to laugh before the speaker delivers it. (Having the audience beat you to the punch really throws your timing to heck. The remainder of the group hears the laughter and you lose the momentum of the joke.) Simultaneously, four or five people will now decide that nothing you have said was true because you lied about this.

The same happens when you falsely portray another's thinking as your own. A woman speaker began quoting Joel Arthur Barker's ideas from his book *Future Edge* as though they were hers. She faced the audience and said importantly, "As I always say, 'If you have paradigm paralysis, you will be hearing nothing but threats (as the next decade offers changes.)'"

Now, that idea certainly was not original with her. You can turn to page 211 in Barker's book and see exactly where he said it. Imagine what could have happened if Barker had been in the audience!

WHAT WILL YOU SAY WHEN THEY ASK YOU PERMISSION TO USE YOUR STORY?

The seminar concludes and you enjoy a tremendous round of applause. A woman works her way to the front of the room to say, "I wanted to tell you I was so delighted with your presentation that I can't wait to go back to work and put it on for my entire office."

What are you going to say? You should be prepared, because it happens all the time. Prepare yourself with this response:

> I'm glad you liked my presentation. I'm sure you'll understand that I am proud of it as well. Therefore, I would love the chance to come present it to your group. I'm sure you didn't mean that you would take the material I worked so hard to create. I did misunderstand you, didn't I?

In addition to the line on your handouts saying that the handout is copyrighted, you might also add, "This presentation in all its forms is the property of (your name). For more information call (your telephone number).

TIP   *Countless speakers have told horror stories about overly enthusiastic introducers who repeat parts of the speaker's presentation. One way to avoid this is to go over your introduction with your announcer verbatim. Explain that you have written this introduction very carefully and exactly.*

Listen carefully to the introduction and be prepared for possible ad libs. One speaker stood at the back of the room in mute horror as the introducer shared 20 minutes of the speaker's best stuff. (The speaker had been invited back for the third year in a row, so the introducer had two years to take notes and practice!)

KNOWLEDGE IS POWER!

The presentation was polished and well done. The speaker moved easily into his closing story, a signature tale about reconciling with his father on his deathbed. Intuitively, the speaker realized that the audience was not with him. Because he was so deep into the story, the speaker had no choice but to continue. The presentation concluded with applause, but the applause was meager compared to the usual response. Later, a participant told the speaker, "Do you realize you are the third presenter at this conference to talk about his dying father?"

Of course, speakers do not present in a vacuum. But how can you be aware of what has happened to your audience before they hear you?

- Ask to come in the day before you present. This gives you the chance to hear other presenters and to talk to your audience.
- Ask for audiotapes of the other presenters who spoke before you arrived. Many conferences tape all the presenters anyway, and a meeting planner who understands the reason behind your request should be happy to comply.
- Talk to the other presenters. What is the topic of their signature stories? What should you share about your presentation? How can you reinforce their messages?

SUMMARY

There are times you should avoid using a story because it doesn't work well on that occasion, it doesn't match you or your audience, or it is out of sync with the mood of the group you are speaking to. You will also want to avoid using stories that are not yours or that are too painful for you to share, and of course, you will not want to tell stories that are offensive or that invade another's privacy. In addition to covering the rules of when not to use a story, we also shared ways to break those rules when speaking. Truth and fiction may mingle freely when you are speaking from the platform, but, most important, keep to the essential truth of a story even if the details are stretched. Finally, work to develop your own signature story so you will have a wonderful story all your own to tell from the platform.

EXERCISES

1. Interview a professional speaker. Ask the speaker about the importance of the ambience that surrounds the speaker's presentation. Ask the speaker how he or she has dealt with problems that cropped up before his or her presentations.

2. Brainstorm the types of last-minute problems that could have an impact on your speech. Include in your list the following:
   - Notice that there is a weather problem.
   - Mention that a friend of the organization has just died.
   - Viewing of a sad video.
   - Announcement of layoffs and job reductions.

3. Discuss how you could find out in advance what the mood of your audience might be.

4. Pretend that another speaker has used your signature story. How will you approach that person? What will you say?

5. Using a story from your life, create fictional details that add to the story's value.

6. A person in your audience walks up to you and says, "Great presentation. I took lots of notes so I can present this myself!" What will you say?

Working with
Your Stories

I am convinced that each work of art, be it a great work of genius or something very small, has its own life, and it will come to the artist, the composer or the writer or the painter, and say, "Here I am: compose me; or write me; or paint me"; and the job of the artist is to serve the work.

Madeleine L'Engle, *Summer of the Great-Grandmother*

Though the timeworn tales of Greece and Rome were fresh and fascinating to them, the Irish monks could occasionally take a dimmer view of their own literature, which we have only because they copied it down, either from childhood memories or from the performance of wandering bards.

Thomas Cahill, *How the Irish Saved Civilization*

HELPING YOUR STORIES GROW

As you work with your stories, you will see them grow and change. You will learn that a slight pause here, a gesture there, an emphasis on a word gives the listener a more enjoyable or heartfelt experience.

Allen Klein, describing a plant leaf his dying wife pasted on a poster of a nude male, originally told the story with a gesture of his hand held low, curling up to suggest the withering of the leaf. Later, he realized the audience could not see the low gesture, so he now gestures above his face.

Drawing on her generous proportions, Liz Curtis Higgs built a funny piece around the Biblical advice, "Your body is a temple of the Holy Spirit." Higgs pointed out God's dilemma, "In my case, He just couldn't decide when to quit building." Over the years, Higgs has developed a new line that never fails to get a chuckle: "Why build a chapel when you could build a cathedral!"

Using your stories regularly, and sharing them with your audiences, exercises your storytelling muscle and provides opportunity to help your stories grow.

THE ILLUSION OF THE FIRST TIME

Ask any speaker what is the most difficult presentation to give, and you will find that giving the same presentation back-to-back two or more times ranks right up there with donating one's brain to science while still alive.

"Didn't I already say that?" you wonder. "Gee, that sounds familiar." (Of course, it does. You said the same thing half an hour ago.)

The crowd laughs at new spots and refuses to crack a smile at the spots that usually bring down the house. Your pacing feels off, and you feel impatient to get the presentation over with.

Unlike an actor with a long-running play on Broadway, you are up there all alone. No one feeds you lines. You don't have the orchestra to sing with. The responsibility for being excited about each and every presentation is yours and yours alone. The challenge of keeping your presentation on track and fresh seems daunting. According to Ellen Dowling in her book *The Standup Trainer*, Konstantin Stanislavsky called "this need for freshness in the midst of repetition 'the illusion of the first time.'" Stanislavsky would know. He was the father of Method Acting, one of the most famous techniques for helping actors achieve their best performances.

The longer you work with your stories, the more familiar they become to you, and the more you must guard yourself from becoming jaded.

INVENTORYING YOUR STORIES

The spotlight turns to you. You walk to the center of the stage and begin to deliver your best story. Suddenly, you realize you've forgotten the order to tell it in—and you feel like an opossum caught in the headlights of an oncoming car. Your eyes open, your mouth sputters, and you feel your mind reaching, reaching, reaching for a shard of the idea that has vanished.

It can happen when you do practice your stories, of course, but it is far more likely to happen when you don't. As your repertoire of stories grows, you'll need to keep track of them. You'll need to be sure that

1. you keep telling the story in the best way possible
2. you don't forget parts of the story
3. you don't forget the best order of elements
4. you remember new twists that work

Using your stories, inventorying them, keeps them where you can reach for them mentally and retrieve them quickly.

Why You Must Inventory Your Stories

Most speakers will want to keep improving their presentations and that often involves replacing old stories with better versions or better stories.

The Japanese call the process of never-ending improvement *kaizen*. When you begin speaking, you may have to use a so-so story to illustrate a point. As you give your presentation, you notice that this particular story works only part of the time. You might also wish you had a story with a different origin, say a business story rather than a personal one. So although you use the so-so story, you continue to cast about for a better story to take its place. This is *kaizen*.

In addition to improving your presentation, you may also wish simply to keep your stock of stories growing so that you have new material for the next presentation you create. Or you may have enough material for one hour and want to be able to speak for one and a half hours if asked. And you may wish to work on new stories in order to keep your presentation flexible so you are able to meet the challenge of appealing to different audiences. Finally, as many of us speakers realize, the stories you hear and see become too precious to lose.

One day I asked my audience, "Tell me about a time when life threw you a curve ball, a time when the Universe had other plans which brought unexpected blessings." A pert woman named Krista responded:

> I had taken my three kids to Payless to go shoe shopping, and we'd come out with seven pairs of shoes. I decided on the way home to stop by the doctor's office and get the results of the tests that had been made.
> You see, I'd had these bruises on my arms and legs that wouldn't go away. I felt perfectly fine. I was sure it was nothing . . .
> It was leukemia.
> I had two questions: (1) What is leukemia? and (2) Will I lose my hair?
> I learned that leukemia is cancer of the blood. I discovered that losing my hair was the least of my worries.
> Well, I had treatments and then last June, I had a bone marrow transplant. Turns out my little brother was a perfect match. And I never thought he was worth much! Guess I better go big for him this Christmas . . . .

My illness changed my whole life and my family and our perspective. Little things don't bother me so much. I don't say yes to everything; I have my priorities straight. Before I was sick, my husband was on every board of every thing. Now he's on just one, and he's closer to our kids in a way he never was before . . . I mean he really knows them now. I guess it was really a blessing. . . .

And now I'm in what they call "recovery," and the doctor tells me that my recovery has been 50 percent attitude. You can see my hair has grown back . . . but it used to be blonde.

The audience sat in total silence. Believe me, there was no story I could have told that day that would have been more important than the message Krista shared.

If I don't remember Krista's story, my audiences will be cheated out of an opportunity to learn and grow from her tribulations. When we speakers forget, when we quit sharing, when we refuse to respect the honor given to us by our audiences, we fail to live up to our potential as speakers and as human beings.

You can't use every good story that comes your way, but you can hold on tight to stories that come to you and continue to look for new homes for them. This year, four of my stories will appear in anthologies. Thank goodness I didn't lose track of them because they are not stories I typically tell from the platform.

How to Inventory Your Stories

Keeping a tab on your stories can be very simple and informal or rather complex. If you only have one presentation with one set of accompanying stories, all you need to do is to keep practicing that presentation. However, if your story inventory grows, you may need to try other ways to keep a handle on the information.

Informal Ways to Inventory Your Stories

- Keep notes of presentations with one-word descriptions to remind you of stories.
- Jot down a couple of key words of stories on index cards.
- List your stories on a piece of paper, using one or two words to jog your memory.

More Formal Ways to Inventory Your Stories

- Tape your presentations with your stories in them.
- Make a tape of your stories.
- Using index cards, write down key points of the stories, sequentially, and punch lines.

Seriously Formal Ways to Inventory Your Stories

- Create a chart for your stories. Note where you use them and audience reaction.
- Have your stories transcribed verbatim.
- Tape your stories and make a list of what you have.
- Create a schedule and a system for reviewing your stories.
- Name each story. Jeff Blackman keeps a list of 187 stories (as of this writing). He has named and checked them off as he presents them in order to be sure he doesn't repeat himself in subsequent engagements for the same client.
- Work up long and short versions of your stories.
- Keep separate lists of stories you feel are perfect, stories that are in progress, and new stories that need work.

TIP *Jeanne Robertson has created her own personal journal in which she records funny or interesting events each day of her life. Besides capturing these moments for later use in her humorous presentations, Robertson also benefits by consciously disciplining herself to practice her skills as a "trained noticer." At regular intervals, Robertson revisits her* *journal pages, deciding what she wants to work on and what has no value.*

Robertson also tracks her use of stories on a large teacher's grade pad. She notes what she uses by presentation and the audience's response. This method helps her to be more aware of stories that have fallen out of use, stories that she wants to work on, and stories that she has yet to use.

TRYING OUT NEW MATERIAL

As we mentioned in the previous chapter, practicing your stories offers an important way to develop your polish as a speaker. Once you have practiced a story, you need to use it in your presentations to see how it fits and how your audience reacts. Tracking your results as you try out new material helps you look at the story objectively, use it safely, and work with it until it reaches its full potential.

Most speakers slip new stories into existing presentations to see how the audience reacts. Obviously, this is a lot less risky than creating an entire presentation of new stuff.

One speaker friend has another idea. She uses showcases and freebies as a place to try her new material: "After all, if I'm not being paid, I'm not cheating them. We both get value and I get the chance to try stuff."

Whether you slip your stories in one by one or give an entire presentation of new material, don't decide to give up on a story if it doesn't do well on its premiere performance. The story might have flopped for a variety of reasons. You may still need practice in telling the new story. Or it might have been a bad match for the audience.

At the least, give the story a couple of tries before you decide to give up on it. Track how it goes and keep tabs as the story develops.

SUMMARY

This chapter covered the essentials of capturing stories and encouraged you to work with your stories on an ongoing basis to improve them. We also discussed the illusion of the first time, the need to make each presentation seem fresh. Several ways of inventorying stories are available to the speaker, and those methods range from the simple and informal to the more complex. The speaker must always be trying out new material.

EXERCISES

1. Revisit a story you told earlier in this book. Tell it again and notice how the story may have changed.

2. Using audio- or videotapes from a professional speaker, see if you can tell how that speaker's stories have changed and grown. Which version of the story do you like best? If the story has changed, why and how has it changed?

3. Try each of the methods listed to inventory stories. Which one do you think will work best for you?

9 Using Humor from the Platform

To be funny in American, you have to be a natural cynic with a tendency toward paranoia. (If you've suffered at the hands of the American medical profession, so much the better.)

Jane Walmsley, *Brit-Think: Ameri-Think: A Transatlantic Survival Guide*

Those of you who do not think you are funny, you are. It would just take a lot more video in your life to find it.

Terry Paulson, National Speakers Association

Humor lets you speak about the unspeakable and allows you to navigate successfully through ticklish situations.

Barbara Mackoff, *What Mona Lisa Knew*

The attempt to develop a sense of humor and to see things in a humorous light is some kind of a trick learned while mastering the art of living.

Viktor E. Frankl, *Man's Search for Meaning*

HOW TO MAKE A SPEECH

"You don't have to be funny to be in the speaking business. Only if you want to get paid," goes the old saying. Today, this witticism rings truer than ever.

Professional speakers are getting more and more entertaining. Modern audiences expect presentations that tickle their funny bones while delivering content, and professional speakers have been forced to rise to the challenge or lose their spot on the podium. An influx of speaking talent coming from the floors of comedy clubs—where making a living is hard and the lifestyle will kill you—has forced once somber speakers to go for jokes. As speaker/business commentator Scott McKain sees the situation, speaking to audiences that were raised on Big Bird, singing and dancing alphabets, and animated dinosaurs and peaches has caused speakers to realize that the speaking business is show business. And, while in show business anything goes for a laugh, speakers and presenters must generate spontaneous eruptions of humor without crossing the line that separates good material from bad taste.

Each year, when the NSA meets for its annual convention, the Humor Professional Emphasis Group (PEG) fills the largest break-out room available. Even speakers who don't call themselves humorists crowd into the Humor PEG room, hoping to pick up a few one-liners as well as tips for turning personal anecdotes into funny stories to be shared from the platform.

To put it mildly, speakers are getting serious about humor. One informal survey asked speakers if they were consciously trying to put more humor into their presentations. The answer was an overwhelming yes. Besides attending the Humor PEG, speakers are working with coaches, practicing with other speakers, reading humor newsletters, and even taking cues from late-night television hosts, all in an effort to jump start the laugh meter.

WHAT IS HUMOR?

The following are some definitions of what humor is.

■ "Humor is exaggeration or surprise." Mark Mayfield
■ "Rebellion against the status quo creates humor." Grady Jim Robinson

- "The ability to see absurdity in our greatest fears." George Valliant, professor of psychiatry at Harvard Medical School
- "Humor is an art. As with any art, increasing awareness enables you to appreciate it more and to improve your skills and talents." Roger Bates
- "Humor helps us shift perspective on our lives. It is a creative alternative to coping with stress." Lorrie Bard, Lola Gillebaard, and Stewart and Jeanne Lerner. (Gee, with all those authors you'd have thought the definition would have been even longer!)

To work with the concept of humor, we need to be more concrete. E. B. White said, "Humor can be dissected as a frog can, but the thing dies in the process." Still, we need to examine humor coolly and logically so that we can recreate it at will. First, here's an all-purpose definition: Humor is the unexpected. Think of the pure hoot of joy a baby gives when she plays peek-a-boo. Her delight springs from the surprise she feels when she learns Mommy didn't really disappear. Our audiences want that thrill. They want to be surprised; they want to witness the BFO (Blinding Flash of the Obvious). And you and I can make that happen.

When we are funny, we take our audiences for a quick ride down a twisty, turny lane, turn a flip, and screech to a halt. Breathlessly, they climb out of the car and holler, "More!"

WHY ALL THE INTEREST IN HUMOR?

Besides the obvious need to meet the entertainment needs of a generation raised on MTV, humor from the platform performs the following functions:

- **It helps the speaker be accepted by the audience more.** The gulf between you and your audience seems as wide as the English Channel until you crack a joke. Suddenly, the folks on the other side realize that (1) you don't take yourself too seriously, (2) you look at life the same way they do, and (3) this is gonna be fun!

■ **It keeps the audience from getting bored.** When you "talk funny," people strain to listen. If they miss a word, they'll miss the punch line. We're rarely bored when we are being entertained. Laughter floods our bodies with oxygen, keeping our minds sharp and focused. "[Humor] gives the audience a breather, a chance to absorb what they are hearing," explains Maggie Bedrosian, author of *Speak Like a Pro.*

■ **It encourages people to have a good time while learning.** Shades of Mary Poppins and her admonition to "take a spoonful of sugar to help the medicine go down." As we laugh, we bring down our defense systems and turn up our curiosities. If we know the time we spend together will be punctuated by laughter, we plan in advance to have a good time. Even difficult material seems easier to comprehend when we relax with humor. You cannot hold tension in your body and laugh at the same time. Better to use our energy comprehending than tensing up. Terry Paulson, author of *They Shoot Managers Don't They?* and *Making Humor Work,* suggests, "By mixing substance with a humorous style, you can get your message across and have the audience enjoy the process."

■ **It makes it easier to share difficult or sensitive material by easing tension and hostility.** If I can get you laughing about sensitive subjects, you put aside your defensiveness and listen. When we laugh together, we admit to life's unpredictability and our own imperfection. When I laugh about myself, I show you that I have learned to accept myself as a fallible human being. As Ethel Barrymore said, "We grow up the day we learn to laugh at ourselves." In the audiotape *The Light Touch,* Malcolm Kushner tells the story of an executive confronted by a hostile employee during a meeting. The employee responded to a remark by the executive with, "You're full of **#$!!" The executive smiled and commented, "You are a very astute person. It takes most people years to realize that about me!" The situation immediately defused.

When we feel comfortable admitting our humanness, we can move out of the shadows of defensiveness and into the glow of understanding. By taking the first step from the platform and laughing at ourselves, although we come before our audiences as "the expert," we lead the way to a higher plane where we can all learn and grow.

- **It improves retention of information.** Because humorous information depends on clever presentation, we follow it more carefully and absorb it on a variety of levels. Paulson reports, "I have had people repeat back some of my anecdotes years after hearing them, and the message is still there working for them as it has for me. Using humor makes your serious points memorable." Humor appeals to our right and left sides of the brain; therefore, the impression made by humorous material has much more staying power than does the impression made by serious material alone. Researcher Joyce Saltman has concluded with others that "humor generally aided in the retention of materials as well as the enjoyment of the presentation of the information."

- **It enhances the creativity of the listener.** Because funny means unexpected, we stretch the listeners' minds. We move from the expected and known to the unknown and unexpected. In the process, our listeners learn new ways to see and process familiar information.

- **It engages the listener's right brain.** Humor appeals to listeners' emotions, and acknowledges the different learning styles we all have. Sharon Bowman plans all her presentations to include both right- and left-brain learning activities, in a method she describes as "honoring all our different learning styles." Most speakers/presenters who deliver content only in a lecture format ignore a part of their audiences by neglecting to appeal to the right-brainers. Humor and storytelling both engage our right brains.

KEY DIFFERENCES: THE HUMOROUS SPEAKER, THE HUMORIST, AND THE COMEDIAN

A comedian's success is judged by the number of laughs per minute he or she receives. In the cold, cruel world of the comedy club, a comedian has seconds to get the audience laughing. Notice, too, that most comedians present one funny bit after another with little or no content or rationale. In fact, the only reason a comedian uses a segue is to keep the audience along for the laughs.

A humorist is a professional speaker whose humor is sanitized for delivery from the platform. A humorist, like a comedian, may tell one funny bit after another with little or no cohesion. A meeting planner who hires a humorist usually expects that the only job of the humorist is to entertain. Although many fine humorists have a message, the message is secondary to the humor. Therefore, a humorist must be funny to maintain the designation.

A humorous speaker is one who enhances his or her content with humor. The humorous speaker gets booked first and foremost because he or she has a topic that interests the meeting planner. Then, the humor becomes an attractive, additional value-added benefit that the speaker offers. A humorous speaker is rarely hired just for the humor.

Figure 9.1 is a rank chart comparing presenters. Note that each presenter is ranked according to content and delivery.

Figure 9.1

RANK CHART

Hired for	Type of presenter	Amount of humor	Amount of content
Entertainment	Comedian	100%, can be blue	None
Entertainment and possibly content	Humorist	75 to 100%, clean	25% or less
Content and possibly entertainment	Humorous speaker	75% or less, clean	25% and up, but topic is important

How can a speaker tell how much content and how much entertainment the presentation should contain? By using a good preprogram questionnaire or by asking appropriate questions in advance of the presentation, the speaker can pinpoint the meeting planner's expectations.

On occasion, a meeting planner might say to a humorous speaker, "We only want content." When this happens to Paulson, he says, "Hey, I only use humor to share content. Otherwise it will be a very, very short program." As you become more comfortable with your own personal speaking style, you'll recognize whether or not humor is an intrinsic part of who you are and what you do or whether you can go without if the situation demands.

HUMOR THAT WORKS AND HUMOR THAT DOESN'T WORK FROM THE PLATFORM

A curious paradox exists concerning humor and the platform. Obscenity abounds in R-rated movies, MTV, and comedy clubs. Over a couple of drinks in the conference-center bar, people's language slides into blue territory and ethnic put-downs blossom like ragweed in August. But from the plat-form, humor must be squeaky clean. Audiences today almost seem to want to catch speakers being offensive.

Mark Mayfield was reminded of this when he was told by an audience member, "You *almost* cussed. I could see you thought about it. We don't allow that, you know. Uh-uh. You would have been in big trouble."

The following four guidelines may help you stay out of big trouble:

1. Never Use Offensive or Scurrilous Language

Years ago, a great controversy loomed at MGM. Should they let Rhett Butler say, "Frankly, my dear, I don't give a damn"?

The mores of the time forbade cursing. Yet, the phrase lost all impact without the offensive word.

How will your audiences feel about cuss words? Better to err on the side of safe than sorry. Purge your vocabulary of *damn* and *hell*. Watch closely for other terms that might be considered offensive.

While blue humor plays well in comedy clubs, from the platform, any off-color commentary can earn you a negative reputation. Meeting planners don't want to apologize to their audiences and board of directors after you leave. If you have any questions about what is acceptable, give it this test: Would I expect to hear a minister or priest or rabbi say this? If it would play in a house of God, take it to work with you.

2. Tiptoe around the Body Functions

Even though you may get away with comments that imply leakage of body fluids, be careful! In one humorist's promotional material, a client said, "I laughed until I wet my pants." Another potential client saw that remark and nixed the humorist as a contender for a presentation at a company get-together.

The point here is NOT what you or I think, but what our audience thinks. While body functions are a normal, natural part of life, and the major conversational component of a discussion with any group of parents, blue-suited business leaders pretend not to have them. Play along.

3. Never Tease Anyone in Your Audience

One school of thought about customizing has long held that you customize by inserting the names of people in your audience into your humorous stories. Right. This is a great idea if you never want to speak again. One speaker did this once with a meeting planner he thought he knew well. The meeting planner was offended, and nothing the speaker could say or do would change the situation. Professional speakers who work with bureaus risk not only offending the client but also causing the bureau to lose a client. The stakes are high, and the payoff is not worth it.

Along the same line, be especially wary of any comment that could be construed as sexual harassment. Don't comment on the attractiveness of a crowd member. Don't tease a man about his stud-muffin attitude. Remember: The people in the audience of your presentation may be there by mandate. This increases the odds that you will be found at fault if they feel they've been sexually harassed. Unlike in a comedy club, these people did not choose to be the brunt of your humor. Therefore, they can more readily portray themselves as victimized if the situation comes to court.

4. Never Ever, Ever Do Ethnic or Religious Humor— Unless You Are Making Fun of Yourself

If you are Irish, you can crack jokes all day about being a leprechaun, or kissing the Blarney stone, but if you aren't, you are making a grave error in judgment. If you do decide to make fun of yourself and your background, make it abundantly clear to your audience that you are laughing at you.

MALE AND FEMALE DIFFERENCES IN HUMOR

A little boy, home from summer camp, once shocked his grandmother by announcing, "Grandma, I know all about sex!" As she caught her breath, he went on to explain that boy rock crabs could be told from girl rock crabs by the shape of their shells.

When it comes to humor, it helps to know "all about sex" by being aware of gender differences in how humor is received.

"Other-directed humor" is the type men most commonly employ. Men grow up learning to compete with each other. Fighting for dominance starts about the time a boy enters kindergarten and continues his entire life. With teasing, men practice their challenges to each other's dominance. Poking fun at another person signals acceptance of that person.

"Self-directed humor" is the primary style that women prefer. Women learn quickly that competition is "not nice," and when one little girl shines in contrast to her peers, she is ostracized. By making fun of themselves, women keep themselves "nonthreatening" and avoid being seen as thinking they are superior. Furthermore, women are taught to be thoughtful and nurturing of others, so laughing at others—particularly those who are weaker—is poor form.

"Situational humor," focusing on the hilarity or awkwardness of the situation rather than of the people involved, offers yet another style of humor. It is the least risky style of humor, because unless the people involved purposely created the situation, it offends no one.

All three types of humor can be planned or spontaneous. When you bring an overhead with a funny picture or saying on it, you have used planned humor. Much of the humor that speakers use on the platform may also seem planned, but it is also possible to plan spontaneous humor by using props or creating a potentially funny situation.

To make sure your humor taps people on the funnybone rather than stabs them in the heart, use self-directed or situational humor. According to Grady Jim Robinson, situational humor that happens in the spontaneity of the moment always brings more laughter than does planned humor. Yet what many speakers fail to realize is that situational humor can be planned to look spontaneous. Mark Mayfield once watched the comic genius Robin Williams do a show in one town. Williams wandered through the crowd, making apparently spontaneous and side-splitting comments about folks' attire, hair styles, and physical appearances. A few days later, Mayfield caught Williams's show in another town, and guess what? Williams walked through the crowd making the same "spontaneous" comments to the new group of people.

TIP *You can create spontaneous humor by rigorously preparing for every situation you encounter as a presenter. Start by listing all the situations you could find yourself in. Here are a few idea generators:*

- missing handouts
- slow service
- quality of the meals
- bad weather outside

Ace comic Dale Irvin is an expert at reducing audiences to howls of laughter with his customarily brilliant use of situational humor. Once, he stepped to the podium after the group was served a minuscule lunch of little more than a few lettuce leaves and shavings from vegetables. Patting his stomach and sucking his teeth, Irvin leaned into the microphone and said, "I don't know about you, but I'm stuffed."

TIP *Humor can help when the unexpected problem occurs. Consider these problems and responses:*

- Microphone doesn't work—"Anybody got an extra megaphone on them?"
- Microphone squeals—"Look out! It's microphone mating season!"
- Lights go out—"Let's join hands and sing Kumbaya!"
- Waiter steps in front of you—"Hi! Are you on the program too?" (Silence.) "Wanna be?"
- Kids screaming in the hall—"Oh, no, will someone go untie my son's babysitter?"
- Short cord on mike—"Did my husband/wife call and ask you to put me on a short leash?"

Handling unexpected problems with light-hearted humor rather than anger will distinguish you as a professional whom meeting planners will want to invite back.

Use the differing styles of humor with care. In a group setting, women will occasionally laugh with men at other-directed humor even when they are uncomfortable about it. Our society has so long told women, "You don't have a sense of humor," that many women have responded by capitulating and becoming disembodied laugh tracks. We don't like it, but rather than be called spoil sports, we laugh about it anyway. Speakers need to note this reaction, because the insensitive speaker who wrings this sort of laughter from the audience will think he or she is doing well, only to discover that a portion of the audience was unhappy. People laugh out of embarrassment as well as out of joy. A speaker can make the audience feel embarrassed—for the speaker—and get a few laughs. But the overall impression the audience gets will not be favorable.

Grady Jim Robinson points out that there are three types of laughter:

- Laughter that is mirth, which is both joyful and freeing. This is laughing "with" someone.
- Laughter that is derisive and puts others down. This is laughing "at" someone.
- Laughter born of embarrassment for the situation another is in. This is laughing "because."

The laughter you want to generate comes from laughing "with" each other.

WHO LAUGHS AND WHEN

The following are a few sweeping generalities about audience composition and their reactions to humor:

■ Predominantly male audiences wearing suits are the least likely to laugh, particularly if the speaker is female.

■ The more serious and left-brain the business, the less likely the audience is to laugh. (Doctors, lawyers, accountants, and Ph.D.s don't laugh. It's a religious oath they took, actually, to take everything seriously.)

■ The more businesslike the setting, the less likely the audience is to laugh.

■ The more distractions going on in the presentation hall, the less likely the audience is to laugh.

■ Alcohol will initially increase the audience's likelihood of laughing, but that quickly plummets. The longer people drink, the later it gets, the more they will laugh with and at each other and the less attention they pay to you.

■ Mixed audiences (male and female) will generally laugh more than predominantly male audiences.

■ Couples will generally laugh more than mixed audiences.

■ The higher the percentage of women in the group, the more likely they will laugh—although once in a while a group of females will have trouble bonding with a female speaker.

■ Male speakers can get away with much more risqué material from the platform than female speakers can. (For example, *hell* and *damn* might be acceptable.)

■ The more artsy the setting, the more accepting the audience will be of risqué material.

■ If the speaker follows bad news, a sad happening, or an unfortunate report on the state of the organization's business affairs, expect little to no laughter. Instead, segue to the humorous portion of your remarks by first acknowledging what the audience might be feeling.

■ In a showcase situation, expect less reaction and certainly less laughter.

■ The less light there is on the speaker, the less people will laugh.

■ The poorer the acoustics or the sound system, the less people will laugh. Try to walk as far into the audience as possible while testing the microphone to see if it whistles or squeals. Ask someone to stand in various parts of the room to make sure you can be heard. Remember, what sounds loud in an empty room will quickly be dampened as the room fills with people. If there will be meal servers in the room, crank the volume up even more.

▪ According to Tom Antion, "The first speaker of the day for an early morning (7 A.M. to 9 A.M.) session should not expect hearty laughter. People are not conditioned to laugh a great deal in the early morning. Many won't even be awake yet."

▪ Antion also notes the hazards of humor outside: "Outdoor presentations are really tough. They are usually full of distractions. The sound systems are inadequate. It is virtually impossible to use overheads or slides." If you do use humor outside, he recommends that you act more animated and really hammer out your punch lines.

▪ Color slides and overheads are funnier than black and white, according to humorist Karyn Buxman.

▪ The more packed the room is, the more laughter you will generate and the longer people will laugh. Laughter is contagious, and it is easier to catch when people are sitting close to each other than when they are sitting in every other seat in a nearly empty room.

▪ Antion also points out that the best seating arrangement for laughter is the semicircle. It allows people to see others around them laughing and encourages them to join in.

▪ People laugh less while they are eating out of fear that they will spray other folks with their masticated food. Humorist Bubba Bechtol prefers not to speak while groups are eating. He worries that an audience member might choke on the food. If you are scheduled to speak over a meal, you might want to talk over this safety concern with the meeting planner.

These generalities are just that: generalities. However, when you know the group's composition, the ambience of the setting, the mode of dress, and time of day, you can better prepare yourself for audience reaction.

SUMMARY

More and more professional speakers are adding humor to their presentations because it keeps the audience interested, makes the speaker more accepted, helps people have a good time, and makes it easier to share sensitive information. The amount of humor in the presentation varies among comedians, humorists, and humorous speakers. Humor must never be used by the speaker if it offends anyone in the audience. Men and women have different humor styles. Audience variables have an impact on how much the audience will laugh.

EXERCISES

1. Watch a comedian, a humorist, and a humorous speaker perform. Note and discuss the differing amounts of humor in their presentations. Can you find the content in the humorist's presentation? Is it obvious?
2. Give examples of the three types of laughter.
3. Tell about a time when someone's attempt at humor backfired and offended you.
4. Observe several types of audiences listening to humorists. Or interview humorists to see which audiences they prefer to work with.
5. What ethnic humor can you use because it is part of your background? How will you alert the audience that you are laughing at yourself?

10 Where to Find Your Sense of Humor

If you practice, you'll eventually start to "think funny."

Ron Dentinger, *Down Time*

Don't be afraid to follow a humorous impulse. It's OK to be spontaneous. . . . Actually the worst that can happen is that no one will laugh. So what? The best thing that can happen is that tension is relieved and they all end up with smiles on their faces and you to thank.

Esther Blumenfeld and Lynne Alpern, *Humor at Work*

People should be taught what is, not what should be. All my humor is based on destruction and despair. If the whole world were tranquil, without disease and violence, I'd be standing in the bread line.

Lenny Bruce, *The Essential Lenny Bruce*

YES, YOU TOO CAN USE HUMOR

Who, me? Yes, you too can use humor, even if you are totally convinced you aren't funny. And even if your topic is serious or content-intense, humor is appropriate.

If your definition of humor covers jokes, puns, and one-liners only, you may have difficulty seeing yourself as someone who can use humor effectively. That's OK, because audiences today don't want to hear your old jokes, or puns, or one-liners. They want you to help them see the humor rampant in your— and their—daily life. Humor is all around us, begging us to enjoy the absurdity of life. As a professional speaker, you guide people into a world where humor abounds.

PLACES TO FIND HUMOR

Once you put up your humor antennae, you discover humor all around you.

- **Travel humor**—The flight attendant giving the safety spiel elicited hoots of laughter when she said, "If you are traveling with a small child, or just someone who acts like a small child, please put on your own oxygen mask first . . . "
- **Printed materials humor**—In the church bulletin: "Join us for our annual burning bowels ceremony . . . "
- **Advertising humor**—On a card extolling the services of a massage therapist: "Body messages."
- **Overheard while waiting in line at a restaurant**— "Work was pretty uneventful last night. Then they brought in a guy who wanted to go fishing and got tired of blowing up his raft boat. He and his buddy took it down to the local gas station and filled it up at the tire air machine. But then it wouldn't fit in the car. So this guy climbs on the car and stretches his arms over the top of the boat, holding it onto the roof while his buddy drives. His wife is following behind them in the other car. Every-thing went all right until a big semi passed them in the opposite lane doing 50 and the draft caused the boat to lift up off the car. Then the guy is airborne. First he flies up in the air. Then, he lands on the trunk of his buddy's car. Finally he crashes onto the road and his wife runs over him! Fortunately his only injury was a broken foot."
- **Overheard in a restaurant as a very chubby little boy talked to his grandmother**—"Grandmother, look! This is my third plate full of food. I can eat almost as much as a human being!"

- **In a magazine**—After socializing together daily for twenty years, eight senior citizens were arrested in Carson, California, when the police raided a "$1-a-game" pinochle party. The player, 64-year-old Sally Rose Lee, had 75¢ on the table at the time of her arrest.

- **From your family**—My seven-year-old son kept staring up at the telephone poles as we were driving in the car. Finally I asked him what he was doing: "Well . . . they call these telephone poles and I'm looking for the telephones on them."

- **At the dog groomer**—"Report card on your dog's behavior: A—I was an angel. B—My halo slipped. C—I just didn't feel like having my hair done. D—I was having a bad hair day. F—I failed completely to see the purpose of this entire exercise."

- **From your friends**—"The doctor was worried that Ted was disoriented after his open-heart operation, so I asked him if he knew who I was and he nodded, 'Yes.' Then I asked him if I could go buy a new Jaguar, and he nodded, 'No.' That's how we knew he was fine."

- **At a kids' soccer game**—A parent brought photos she had taken of the team last year. One picture showed a group of kids chasing the ball while in the end zone near the goal, two team members stood side by side looking together at a dandelion.

If you notice the absurdity of the world around you, you will always have plenty of great humorous raw material to work with. Best of all, this sort of homegrown humor usually plays well with audiences because they too have lives in which humor abounds.

SENSITIZING YOUR HUMOR ANTENNAE

If humor exists all around us, why do we often overlook funny stuff? Just like in finding stories, we must be sensitized to the humor around us.

You can sensitize yourself by learning to "think funny."

1. **Ask yourself, "How would this situation look if it were exaggerated?"** Remember the old joke, "It was so cold that . . . ?" Ask yourself how the situation could be worse, or better, or bigger, or smaller.

2. **Ask yourself, "What would surprise me?"** You know what is expected. Now, consider the unexpected. Use synergy to create a surprise in an expected situation. For example, think about how cartoon characters introduce themselves. Remember Ricochet Rabbit? He used to announce himself by saying, "I'm . . . Ping . . . Ping . . . Ping . . . Ricochet Rabbit." Now, conjure up a situation where you would be expected to give your name calmly. How about when waiting for a table at a restaurant? What would people expect? A calm recitation of your name. What would surprise them? "I'm . . . Ping . . . Ping . . . Ping . . . Ricochet Rabbit."

3. **Scan newspapers, magazines, and all sorts of printed materials looking for the interesting and the absurd.** In *Speak Like a Pro,* presentation expert Maggie Bedrosian suggests looking for humor in the *Wall Street Journal.* "It is a powerful source of humor," she explains, "because most people don't expect it to be funny."

4. **Ask other people about what funny stuff has happened to them.** An airport shuttle bus driver once told this story about a television star who rode his bus. Mr. Star said to the shuttle driver, "Don't you know who I am?" When the shuttle driver admitted he didn't, Mr. Star said, "I'm on TV. Want my autograph?" The shuttle driver said, "No, thank you." Mr. Star said, "Oh, come on! You don't get a chance like this every day." Again, the shuttle driver said, "No, thank you." Finally, they reached their destination and Mr. Star pulled a glossy photo from his briefcase and signed it with a flourish. "I understand," said Mr. Star, "you were just too shy to ask!"

5. **Eavesdrop.** You'll hear incredible stuff. Make sure you don't choke on your cola and give away that you were listening. Be covert!

6. **Revisit a tragedy.** At the time, discovering that the dog ate the Thanksgiving turkey seemed like a tragedy. But time heals. Today your dog's epicurean misadventures seem funny.

7. **Watch the comedy masters on late-night television.** Late-night television hosts Jay Leno and David Letterman use jokes each night compiled by an entire staff of joke writers. Do not try to steal their material and use it for yourself. Do listen and learn. How did they make that news item funny? How did they combine two topics to create a humorous and unexpected comment?

8. **Read.** *Reader's Digest* has numerous sections devoted to humor. Again, do not steal these anecdotes. Because you are stealing from the world's most widely read magazine, the chance is good that your audience has already seen this humor. But the more humor you read, the more you learn about structuring material in funny ways. Also consider reading humorous books. Dave Barry, Art Buchwald, Jeff Foxworthy, the late Erma Bombeck and the late Lewis Grizzard have compiled their materials into books that offer a neophyte speaker page after page of great ideas about humor. Lawrence Sanders and Carl Hiaasen do not write books of humor, but their characters are side-splittingly funny. You may glean a one-liner from either that will work well in your presentations.

9. **Listen to tapes of the great humorists.** Jeff Foxworthy, Bill Cosby, Carl Hurley, Ralph Hood, and Liz Curtis Higgs all sell audiotapes. Again, don't steal their material, but use it to start those spark plugs firing in the humor section of your brain.

10. **Listen to the radio.** *Car Talk, A Prairie Home Companion,* and *What Do You Know?* can be heard on your local public radio station. For good clean humor, these shows take first prize. *Car Talk* and *What Do You Know?* give great examples of spontaneous humor in action. One *What Do You Know?* program featured a woman who was called at random by host Michael Feldman. After Feldman questioned her about her life and her town, she

commented, "Well, it was nice talking to you but I have some other things to do, so I'll have to go now." What a terrific example of the unexpected! With millions of listeners all over the globe who would give away first-born children to talk with Feldman, he managed to find the one person who'd rather do her laundry than chat.

11. **Go see a humorist or a comedian.** Scan your local newspapers for notes about organizations that are bringing humorists to town. Read the ads of comedy clubs and plan a date to hear a comedian. Don't steal their material, but do bring a notepad and write down stuff that strikes you as funny. Can you think of a similar situation? Can you see comic patterns? Did the humorist/comedian create characters? If so, what were the distinguishing features of the characters? If you get to see several presenters in a row, compare and contrast their comic styles.

12. **Watch movies.** Watch the new and brightest stars, Jim Carrey and Eddie Murphy, as well as those who have had longer careers, Lily Tomlin, Bette Midler, and Goldie Hawn. Don't forget the classics, Jerry Lewis, Red Skelton, Bob Hope, and Red Buttons. Again, look for humor patterns.

13. **Watch television.** Sit-coms (situation comedies) rely on predictable patterns of behavior to be funny. Yes, you can learn about humor by watching, but the humor will have limited use because you are not an established character who can rely on your audience's knowledge of you to create humor. Still, television does use humor, and you can learn about what works by watching.

14. **Watch the old masters.** As a child, I heard the stories of hometown hero Red Skelton and his rise to comedic fame. At night, watching Skelton on television, my father would laugh hysterically over Skelton's characters: Freddy the Freeloader, Gertrude and Heathcliffe, and The Mean Little Kid. You can buy tapes of old television shows with masters like Skelton, Jackie Gleason, and Jack Benny. They are well worth your time and money.

15. **Listen to the old-time radio humor masters on audiotapes.** These tape-recordings of the popular shows

of yesterday can help you fine-tune your sense of humor while you enjoy the laughter of another day. In *How to Be Funny,* Steve Allen says, "I attach particular importance, in this connection, to watching and listening to recorded humor. Not only can you enjoy it the first time, but the experience can be easily repeated, which is especially helpful if your intentions are analytical."

16. **Enjoy the comics in the newspapers.** These offer you visual pieces you can include in overheads, but not in duplicated handouts. According to copyright expert Mike Rounds, displaying a comic strip or cartoon as an overhead or slide does not violate the copyright law. However, reprinting a comic strip or cartoon on your handouts, faxes, or newsletters does. Besides using the cartoons in your presentation, you can also refer to what you've seen by describing the cartoon. And, of course, exposing yourself to the humor of the cartoonist also works to sharpen your own sense of humor.

17. **Subscribe to a humor newsletter.** These publications offer humor you can use. If you don't use their bits, you can still generate new ideas by reading these newsletters. Different publications specialize in different types of humor, so ask for a sample copy before subscribing. See my resource list for names and phone numbers.

18. **Collect joke books.** On occasion you may wish to resurrect an old joke. Audiences will forgive you if they haven't heard the joke millions of times before. Again, the joke books benefit you most by exposing you to humor. Look for patterns, substitute words that would fit your messages, and try to create your own humor.

19. **Join the National Speakers Association and its Humor PEG.** You'll meet others who share the desire to keep audiences laughing. PEG meetings allow members to discuss new ideas and resources. The PEG newsletter, published four times a year, also keeps members up to date on new ideas, tips, techniques, and resources for humor.

20. **Surf the net for humor.** Go to the Internet and use the word *humor* to search. Also try *comedy, wit,* and *jokes.* Also check out www.infobahn.com/pages/anagram.html. This site instantly turns whatever you enter into anagrams.

21. **Hire a humor coach.** Once you find a humorist you admire, find out if he or she offers coaching services. Prices will vary, and how these coaches work will also differ. Discuss in advance what your expectations and goals are. If you aren't near a humorist, consider putting together a consortium of others who want to work on their humor skills and chipping in to bring a humorist to town.

22. **Collect books that tell you how to create humor.** None of these books will work unless you take them off the shelves and actually complete the exercises. After all, you didn't learn to ride a bike by reading about bike riding, did you?

23. **Hang around funny people.** Let's face it. I have friends who are a hoot and friends who need one. Some people naturally tickle our funny bones. Sure, I learn a lot from all my friends, but the humorous ones encourage me to try my best stuff on them. And that improves my H.Q. (humor quotient).

24. **Buy a prop.** Find a prop that works well for you and use it consistently. Karyn Buxman waves a magic wand and pops on a clown nose. Props are available through catalogs and in retail stores. Spencer Gifts offers funny props, and at Halloween you can find strange hats, masks, and accessories at party goods stores and other specialty shops.

25. **Hang around kids.** They get tickled about the silliest stuff. If we could only learn to see our world with their sense of wonder, how much happier we'd all be.

26. **Look for signs.** A parking lot of an engineering firm boasts this gem: *Entrance by employees or visitors prohibited.* So who gets to park here, anyway? The tooth fairy?

THE BEST SOURCE FOR HUMOR . . .

Is your life. When we look at our lives with an eye toward the irony, we lighten up. Liz Curtis Higgs describes her book *Only Angels Can Wing It: The Rest of Us Have to Practice* as offering "therapeutic humor, the kind that comes from real life, not joke books." Jeanne Robertson notes that women humorists have always taken their cues from real life, not from gags and joke books.

Real-life humor beats any joke you can tell, anytime, hands down. When we have the opportunity to view our lives through the lens of humor, we feel closer to each other and more in control. Real-life humor reminds us not to take ourselves too seriously. As Robertson says, "we want to see ourselves, thus we do," and although she is talking about seeing ourselves in the characters of "The Andy Griffith Show," she also points to the larger metaphor of seeing ourselves as real people, in real life, dealing with real funny situations.

As we hear a funny story and think, "That could have happened to me," we reassure ourselves that we are one with our fellow human beings, slugging it out here on the third rock from the sun. Notice how similar these words are: *humor* and *human.* The commonality of our experience makes real life the best source ever for humor.

WHEN DO YOU USE HUMOR FROM THE PLATFORM?

By now, you are probably seeing the humor all around you. You've convinced yourself of the truth: Life is a running gag. So you think you might be ready to put your humorous pieces to work. Well, first check the following list of guidelines.

1. Does Your Humor Support a Point?

A speaker told this story: A little boy ran to his mother sobbing, "Mommy, Mommy! There's someone under my bed." His mother said, "Honey, what on earth are you talking about?" The little boy answered, "Remember when the preacher said from dust you came and to dust ye shall return? Well, someone is under my bed and I don't know whether he's coming or going." Then the speaker launched into a story on customer service. Puzzled looks appeared on the faces of the audience as it struggled to find the correlation between the dust balls and customer service.

If your humor makes a point, it supports your ideas and helps your audience move from one thought to the next. Pointless humor confuses the audience. Worse, when pointless humor bombs, you look really silly because your comments had no purpose at all. As Patricia Ball explains in *Straight Talk Is More Than Words,* "Use high-impact humor sandwiches. Tell your audience the point you intend to make, then tell the story or joke to illustrate the point, then repeat the point."

2. Does Your Humor Complement You?

We all have personal style. Some humorous bits—usually stolen ones—simply don't match our personae. When we are authentic and credible, our messages come across loud and clear. You can use your persona as a foil to create laughter when there exists an unusual juxtaposition of who you are and what you share. However, this still must be in keeping with your personal style and your audience's style. For women presenters, this is particularly crucial. Audiences hold women to much higher standards of conduct than they do men. Experts suggest that this is because our society wants the mothers of its children to stand for all that is good and right and pure. And so a woman who tells a story more suited to the barroom than the boardroom risks ruining her credibility and offending the audience. Of course, it goes without saying that men can also use humor in an offensive way.

3. Does Your Humor Match the Needs of Your Audience?

Every audience is different. By using a preprogram questionnaire, you can tailor your remarks and your information to each audience's needs and culture. One executive who had recently moved to Australia neglected to preview his speech with other corporate officers who had spent more time "down under." During his stirring keynote urging the entire corporation to operate as a team, he said, "I'm so proud of who we are and what we represent that I've ordered fanny packs embroidered with our corporate logo for each of you to wear!" The audience sat in stunned silence. Then a few pockets of embarrassed giggles surfaced. Finally the entire crowd rocked with laughter. Only later did the executive discover his faux pas. In the United States, fanny packs are hip-hugging, zippered pouches used like purses to carry keys, spare change, and so on. In Australia, fanny packs are feminine hygiene products.

You might also miss your audience's needs by neglecting to consider members' ages, incomes, and educations. You certainly don't want to talk down to anyone. But laughing about problems you've had getting your full-length mink hemmed will not win you any points with folks who are struggling to make ends meet.

If your audience is different from you in age, tell them what someone in their age group has to say. A wise speaker won't make jokes about growing old when he talks to a group of seniors. He can, however, tell them what his mother has to say about growing old.

4. Does the Humor Relate to Their Industry?

Mark Mayfield says, "Never tell a lawyer joke to a bunch of attorneys in an attempt to customize your humor, because they've heard every joke about a lawyer ever written." Furthermore, the line between tickling and offending here is far too blurred for comfort.

You can relate humor to an industry by making your anecdote happen to one of them. So, for example, you could tell them about the lawyer neighbor of yours with the t-shirt that says, "If you think talk is cheap, call an attorney." As Mark Mayfield suggests, "Don't make it industry specific; make it personal."

TIP *Let your humor shine in your correspondence, answering machine message, and marketing. Funny guy and speaker Scott Friedman sent this postcard out to his clients shortly after New Year's Day:*

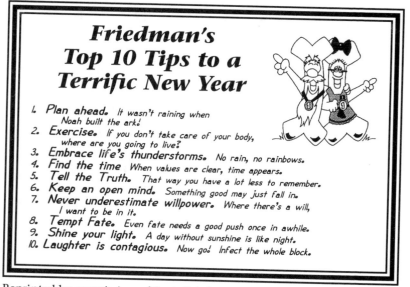

Friedman's Top 10 Tips to a Terrific New Year

1. **Plan ahead.** It wasn't raining when Noah built the ark!
2. **Exercise.** If you don't take care of your body, where are you going to live?
3. **Embrace life's thunderstorms.** No rain, no rainbows.
4. **Find the time** When values are clear, time appears.
5. **Tell the Truth.** That way you have a lot less to remember.
6. **Keep an open mind.** Something good may just fall in.
7. **Never underestimate willpower.** Where there's a will, I want to be in it.
8. **Tempt Fate.** Even fate needs a good push once in awhile.
9. **Shine your light.** A day without sunshine is like night.
10. **Laughter is contagious.** Now go! Infect the whole block.

Reprinted by permission of Scott Friedman, motivational humorist.

By using his humor in his correspondence, Friedman reminded his contacts that he is a very funny guy.

WHAT DIFFERENT TYPES OF
HUMOR ARE THERE?

Let's define our terms by listing and explaining the different forms that humor takes.

1. **Joke.** A made-up story about stereotypes or famous people. Most jokes have no point other than to entertain. For example, "I once knew a man who died of a cough. Of course, he was found in another man's closet at the time."

2. **One-liner.** A funny saying or comment. These may be used to emphasize a point or simply to entertain. Also called a quip. Wendy's, the fast-food outlet, became famous for a commercial that featured two little old ladies examining their sandwiches and asking, "Where's the beef?" The line went on to have a life of its own, entering popular culture as a way of asking, "So what's the import?"

3. **Punch line.** The climactic phrase or sentence that turns the situation or set-up on its ear and creates the humor. Here's a classic:

   Knock, knock.
   Who's there.
   Boo.
   Boo who?
   Why are you crying?

   The punch line is "Why are you crying?"

4. **Punch word.** The climactic word that turns the situation or set-up around and creates the humor. For example, I tell my audiences about the time we moved seven times in three years. I knew I was getting hard to live with, but I didn't realize how bad I had become. Then, for Christmas, I opened a present and found inside a full-color brochure for an expensive health spa. The copy said, "Here is the perfect place to rejuvenate your

body and refresh your spirit." I said to my husband, "Oh, honey, this must have been expensive." He said, "Not really. People chipped in." The punch words are *chipped in.* Notice the use of hard consonant sounds. Notice also how short and snappy those two words are.

5. **Set-up.** The situation that provides the background to the joke. A set-up starts the listener down the path by giving the background material necessary to make the joke funny. In the previous anecdote, the set-up is the explanation of how grouchy I had become and why.

6. **Stacking.** When one punch line or punch word follows another, building the humor value as they go, this is called "stacking."

> My husband was flipping through a magazine when he came upon a picture of Demi Moore in the outfit she wore in *Striptease.* "With a little bit of work," he said, "you could look just like this." (The audience usually snickers and groans here.) So I flipped to a picture of Bruce Willis, and I said, "See this? No matter how much you work, you'll never look like this." (Pause.) "Ever."

By stacking one funny comment on another, you build on the laughter.

7. **Call-back.** Repeating a funny line or word later in the presentation to evoke more laughter. If later in the presentation, I sigh and shake my head and say, "No matter how much you work . . . ," chances are the audience will laugh with me as they remember the joke.

8. **Bit.** An enlarged funny sketch, anecdote, joke, or series of one-liners. Tom Antion, author of *Wake 'em Up Business Presentations,* describes a bit as "a section of material that is so related that it makes it easy for you to memorize."

Remember the classic Bud Abbott–Lou Costello routine, "Who's on First?" With its stacking of one punch line after another, this classic perfectly exemplifies a bit. Bits are useful because they help us build our material. If your presentation is running too long, simply leave out or condense a bit. Working through your material in bits also helps you memorize your work. Antion explains, "I practice the bit over and over until I can do it in my sleep. When the presentation comes, all I have to do is remember the set-up line . . . and those key words trigger the bit."

9. **Straight man or straight woman.** The person who delivers the set-up. When George Burns and his wife Gracie Allen began their comic career, Gracie was the straight person and George delivered the funny lines. However, their career really caught on when they reversed the situation.

10. **Funny man.** The person who delivers the punch line or punch word. A great example of a straight man and a funny man are the Smothers Brothers, a popular comic duo who later had their own television show. Dickie, the older brother, would make a comment, and Tommy would respond with a funny line, which eventually culminated in a bickering session. The call-back was Tommy whining, "Mother always liked you best."

11. **Pun.** Wordplay for the sake of humor. For example, Grady Jim Robinson tells a story about a boy who came to the Christmas play dressed in a firefighter's outfit. When asked why he was wearing the boots and overcoat, the boy replied, "Well . . . the Bible says the Three Wise Men came from afar (a fire)." (Grady really uses his Southern accent to advantage here!)

    Michael Iapoce notes that the laughter generated by puns "is given up grudgingly. This is because by its very nature, a pun is a statement of how clever one is—how much more clever than the audience!" Puns should be used sparingly.

12. **Props.** "Prop" is short for "property," a physical item used in a stage production. Props for humor might include funny hats, glasses with fake noses, red clown noses, funny shoes, and other toys. Speaker and chiropractor Jenna Eisenberg opens what she calls her "perspective box," a purple plastic container crammed with items that prompt her to tell stories designed to maintain a positive perspective. One example is a photo of a little girl who slapped a play $20 bill into Jenna's hand and announced, "And this is for you, Eisenberg."

13. **Gag.** A joke or one-liner. Gilda Radner cracked up audiences by telling them the name of her character "Roseanne Roseanna Danna."

14 **Slapstick.** Physical humor which usually involves some sort of faked harm to the humorist, like a pie in the face.

TIP *If you don't have a Southern accent, get one.*
Seriously, humorists laugh about the fact that a Southern accent seems funnier than, say, a Boston one. One theory is that most of us think people who talk with a Southern accent are, ahem, challenged in the IQ department. Of course, that's not true. Yours truly was born in Florida and there's nothing wrong with my IQ that a few extra numbers wouldn't help. We do know that most folks like to feel superior, and Southern humorists suspect they have an advantage because their audiences hear the accent and think, "This person can't put one over on me!" Surely the great success of "Mayberry RFD," and "The Andy Griffith Show" may have convinced us that Southerners are gentle with their humor. And it's infinitely easier to laugh when we don't feel threatened.

Brooklyn accents can also be funny, but in a more aggressive way. If you have one, slow down a bit, please, because those of us from the South can't keep up. (Most Northerners do talk faster than Southerners. When you talk too fast, your humor doesn't have time to make an impact. Slow down.)

Perhaps the truth is that we simply listen more expectantly when we hear an unfamiliar pronunciation. Whatever, if you have a bit of Southern twang, keep whistling Dixie and thank those lovely stars that make up the Southern Cross.

IN CASE OF EMERGENCY: READ THIS BEFORE YOU TROT OUT YOUR FUNNY STUFF

You are not truly prepared to work on humor in your presentation until you know what to do when your humor bombs.

No matter how good you are, no matter how polished your humor is, every audience is different.

One meeting planner was startled by how differently three audiences perceived the same repeated presentation. After introducing the speaker, the meeting planner stayed in the room for the entire presentation. "I can't believe how different each group was," she commented. "They all laughed at different points in the presentation."

Each group has its own chemistry. The make up of the attendees, the effect of the presentation they heard before you spoke, the intimacy of the room, and the time of day also change how they view your material. Larry Wilde, an author of 53 joke books and a former stand-up comedian, says that Bob Hope used to bring in a new audience in lieu of trashing his material. Imagine that! Hope believed in his material even when his audiences didn't.

So what's a speaker to do? We need to be prepared when our material bombs. Here are three rules to keep you out of trouble:

1. **Never start a presentation with a joke.** If it falls flat, you have set the tone for the rest of your talk. You have too much riding on the first few minutes of your presentation to set yourself up for failure. Besides the audience's poor first impression, you will have to deal with your emotions after you bomb.

2. **Never start a joke by telling people, "Here is a joke . . . "** First, you've set up their natural inclination to be skeptical about how funny you are. Second, if it falls flat they know you've failed. And last but not least, it sounds so amateurish that folks are likely to roll their eyes in disgust.

3. **Never write out a joke and read it.** "The funniest story will fall flatter and colder than yesterday's pancake if it is read," says James C. Humes in his book *Standing Ovation.* An exception is when you pretend to read funny

stories that have appeared in the news while holding the news source.

The following are seven suggestions that will also help you use humor with panache.

1. Keep Your Funny Stuff Short—So You Can Bail Out

Short material moves quickly. If you get into a long, drawn-out anecdote and you lose the crowd, you can't quit even though you know you've lost it. This guideline is one developed from the experiences of Mark Mayfield. One time, Mayfield launched into a long story, not realizing that the speaker immediately before him had stolen his anecdote. By the time Mayfield was deep into his tale, he realized the group wasn't with him, and it was too late to bail out. A few seconds can seem like a lifetime when you've lost the attention of an entire room full of people.

In his book *A Funny Thing Happened on the Way to the Boardroom: Using Humor in Business Speaking,* Michael Iapoce suggests that you always cut the number of words in your jokes and stories. "Jokes are a lot like poetry: You want to get a maximum impact from a minimum of words," he explains.

Presenters often tell too much when they tell a joke or anecdote. Ask yourself, "If I cut this, does it matter? Does it change the essential meaning of the joke?" Voltaire once said, "The secret of being a bore is to tell everything." Don't tell your audience any more than it must know to understand the punch line of your anecdote.

2. But Don't Bail Out of Your Entire Presentation

Audiences may take a while to warm up and relax, but you'll never know if you bail out and cancel the humorous part of your presentation due to lack of interest. Iapoce says, "Whatever happens, don't start making on-the-spot revisions in your planned material if the first joke or two doesn't work! This means you shouldn't drop, add, or change any of the humor you were going to use, or you'll end up destroying all the careful preparation you put into it (and if you *haven't* prepared carefully, you're probably getting what you deserve.)"

Occasionally, the group will wait to see who else is laughing before the rest decide to join in. Tom Antion says, "One of the hardest audiences to deal with consists of a group of executives from the same company when the CEO is present. If you say something funny, the executives will start to laugh, but they choke it off until they check to see if the CEO is laughing." This also happens in other groups where there are strong-influence leaders. People will look around nervously before they laugh.

Iapoce notes that "the audience may not get the idea that they're supposed to laugh after only one joke." Again, they need time to conclude that (1) laughter is allowed and (2) you're going to keep on being funny *on purpose* until they join in.

3. Support a Point, and It Doesn't Have to Be Funny

After all, it supported the point you were making. Whether it was funny or mildly amusing doesn't matter if the information had intrinsic value. Terry Paulson says, "Effective speakers are not necessarily humorists, but they can use humor. Their humor is used to support and illustrate their central message."

4. Have a Few Snappy Come-Backs Ready

What will you do when they stare blankly at you? Be prepared like the professional comedians are by having a "saver" or two at the ready:

- "My mother didn't like that one either!"
- "That's funny, my dog laughed like a hyena at that!"
- "No, well, I didn't think that was funny either . . . "
- "Please check the person next to you and make sure he or she is breathing."
- "Gee, are you all secretly accountants or bankers? They never laugh either."
- "Well, I guess I'll have to fire my joke writer. That means my husband/wife is gonna have to go out and get a real job."
- "Oh, go ahead. Take a walk on the wild side and snicker. You can do it."

TIP *When you watch the great humorists perform, you are immediately struck by their level of assurance. They believe they are funny. They exude confidence as they walk on the stage. They deliver their lines and wait for the audience to respond. Eventually, the audience has no choice but to join in.*

5. Keep Your Energy Level Up, and Don't Let the Group Bring You Down

Once your energy level starts to drop, you can't perform as effectively as you would like. Yes, speaking is a performance skill. Even the most natural of presenters are performing. Our audiences sense our changing energy patterns. Don't let yourself get caught up in a spiral of self-doubt just because they didn't laugh at a few of your bits. While you are worrying over your last piece, they are ready, willing, and able to laugh at your next remark.

6. Find Their Funny Bone and Tickle It

They didn't laugh where you thought they would, but they laughed uproariously when you knocked the flip chart over.

Hey, they're trying to tell you: "Get physical." Or they didn't laugh at the prop you brought, but they busted a gut when you talked about being mistaken for an EMT. They're telling you they like comedy where someone is confused. Listen to them. Your audience wants to tell you how to entertain them.

7. Be Conversational in Your Delivery

Iapoce points out, "There are many jokes that may read funny in a joke book, but sound stilted and decidedly unfunny when you attempt to repeat them as they were written." Don't use words you wouldn't normally use in everyday speech.

NEVER-FAIL HUMOR—DOES IT REALLY EXIST?

No. However, you will find that parts of your presentation do typically bring a positive response. One group laughs out loud. Another chuckles. And the last one only smiles delightedly. We don't all have the same response to humor . . . and that doesn't mean we didn't enjoy what we heard.

How we respond to humor depends largely on our personal styles.

- **Open and outgoing with a task orientation.** These folks take their fun seriously. They laugh loud and heartily, turning to others in the crowd and urging them to laugh too. Although it takes a while to win this group over, once they are on your side, they'll stick with you. You'll know you have them when they uncross their arms. Be ready for them to tease you back, too. These people are entrepreneurs, business owners, managers, and successful sales people.
- **Open and outgoing with a people orientation.** Life is a continual party for these people. As long as they like you, and as long as they have a reason to be in a good mood, they will enjoy just about everything you say. In

fact, they will snort and leak body fluids while being entertained. These folks get so amused they literally fall off their chairs. Be sure to leave them plenty of time to get themselves back in control before you set them off again. Sales people, other speakers, writers, customer service representatives, nurses, teachers, and counselors tend to be open and outgoing with a people orientation. Expect a standing ovation from these folks.

- **Quiet and reserved with a people orientation.** Gentle and kind, this group will be the most offended if your humor is at all hurtful. On the other hand, they will snicker quietly even if you botch your bits. But, beware: they may only feel sorry for you. Expect them to warm up to laughter slowly but to smirk and giggle throughout your presentation. These folks are likely to be staff people, office workers, some retail clerks, stay-at-home wives, food service workers, volunteers, and other behind-the-scene laborers who keep the world running along smoothly.

- **Quiet and reserved with a task orientation.** Unless your humor has a point, they'll pass, thank you. To these people, the bottom line is everything. Your humor must be short, crisp, and to the point. Although their laughter is infrequent, they may be amused. It's hard to tell. Listen to this group carefully for one-liners and zingers that will be much funnier than anything you have to share. Their observations on human nature have been honed to a razor-sharp edge, and their comments will be terse and right-on-target. You'll generally find these people in the accounting department, working with computers, and handling detail work.

STAYING ON THE
SAFE SIDE OF HUMOR

In his book *Standing Ovation: How to Be an Effective Speaker and Communicator,* James C. Humes suggests that all humor should pass the three R test: Realistic, Relevant, and

Retellable. Humor that is too far-fetched doesn't pass the test for realism. Humor without a point fails the test for relevant. Humor that might offend anyone in the group flunks the test for retellable.

What is retellable for me may not be retellable for you. Context provides the key. In this case, the context includes the background of the speaker, the bond established with the group, and the use of the story to make a point.

Humes, a former speech writer for presidents, points out that the greater the celebrity of a speaker, the higher the likelihood that people will laugh at the speaker's jokes. Or as Humes explains, "President Reagan gets laughs because he is the president!" The persona of the celebrity creates a comic foil, a new context for the joke.

When I wrote speeches for the executives of Diamond-Star Motors, I learned this lesson too well. I asked a meeting planner to tell me what subject he wanted the chairman of Diamond-Star to address. "Lady," he groaned, "I don't care what he says. Frankly, I don't care if he comes and drops his pants. All that matters is that I got the chairman of Diamond-Star Motors to come to our event."

The halo effect of celebrity casts a glow that you and I may not have as professional speakers. When we talk, we will be judged much more harshly. Therefore, if you are ever in doubt about your humor, leave it out. The risk is too great, and the reward is too small.

SUMMARY

Expand your definition of humor so that even if you cannot tell a joke, you can be funny on the platform. Be sure to pay attention to the funny observations you make about life all around you. By actively looking for humor, exposing yourself to humor, and paying more attention to daily life, you will increase your ability to be funny on the platform. To be effective, humor must match your personality and the group's needs, relate positively to the group's industry, and support a point. Never start a presentation with a joke, never "announce" the joke, and never read a joke if you want to be funny. Different types of people will respond differently to humor, so be aware of your audience and yourself, and test your humor before you present it.

EXERCISES

1. Create a presentation using humor. Include humor from a variety of sources in your everyday life.
2. Choose three or four ways to expose yourself to more humor. Which yielded the most improvement in your sense of humor? Why?
3. Talk with classmates or colleagues about the ways they exposed themselves to humor. What helped them find the lighter side of life? Why?
4. Share with your group an unexpected source of humor in your life.
5. Discuss various snappy come-backs to common speaking problems and create your own list of them.

11 Creating Humor

If I can get you to laugh with me, you like me better, which makes you more open to my ideas. And if I can persuade you to laugh at the particular point I make, by laughing at it you acknowledge its truth.

John Cleese, quoted in *Quotations to Cheer You Up When the World is Getting You Down* by Allen Klein

Comedians know how to be funny because they practice; but if you want to see funny, you need to practice too.

Allen Klein, *The Healing Power of Humor*

*Humor is a prelude to faith and
Laughter is the beginning of prayer.*

Reinhold Niebuhr, *Discerning the Signs of the Times*

Humorists also have a built-in tendency to see and enjoy the incongruities, ironies, absurdities, and ridiculous aspects of real life. They thrive on the oddities of things that happen . . .

Paul E. McGhee, *How to Develop Your Sense of Humor*

GET FUNNY. NOW.

We've covered what humor is, where to find humor, when to use humor, and how to minimize the risks you take when you use humor. Now all you have to do is get funny.

Like all skills, being funny can be learned. The best humorists and comedians are ardent students of their craft. They don't just listen to a joke; they analyze why it does or doesn't work. Because good humorists take the time to learn about their craft, they improve. Take heart. You too can learn and improve.

THE SHAPE OF HUMOR

If you could draw a picture of humor, it would look like an exclamation mark turned upside down and tilted (see Figure 11.1). The body or set-up of the humor is short, full, and slants upward. Then comes a slight pause, the space between the body of the exclamation mark and the dot. Finally, the dot represents the explosive power of the punch word. Note that the dot is disconnected from the body. This happens because the punch word or punch line surprises the listener. There is a bit of a disconnect because the punch line or punch word must be unexpected, a non sequitur.

If you review the art of crafting a story, you will quickly note that a humorous piece works the same way: there is a setting of the stage, characterization may occur, and the climax is the punch line or punch word. So how can humor be so difficult to deliver?

Figure 11.1

THE SHAPE OF HUMOR

Punch Line or
Punch Word

Set-up

FAILINGS OF WOULD-BE HUMORISTS

1. **The set-up is too long.** Terry Paulson explains that the average length of a story or a joke is about 15 seconds. Larry Wilde notes, "If you can't hit oil in 20 seconds, stop boring." Take a stop watch to your humor. If it goes longer than 30 seconds, you've lost the element of surprise.

2. **The punch word wasn't at the end of the bit.** James C. Humes explains, "A joke demands the *build-up* of tensions and the release of tension to cause the *burst* of laughter." Think of the punch word or trigger word as the pin that bursts the balloon. Obviously, if you wait until the balloon fills to its capacity, the pop will be much more satisfying. Remember the old joke, "Take my wife. Please!" The impact would be lost if it were reversed: "Please take my wife."

3. **The punch word isn't funny.** Mark Mayfield notes that hard consonants are funnier than soft. "So, Betsy is funnier than Susan," he explains. He's right. Double-check your punch word to see if you can substitute a word with hard consonants.

4. **The punch word isn't short enough.** Shorter is better. "Men tell me that women shouldn't complain so much about pantyhose. 'After all,' said one man, 'we have to shave.' Hey . . . I'm here to tell you I've shaved places you guys would never go near . . . with a razor." *Razor* is the punch word and has to be spoken very distinctly. In fact, I always pause (as indicated by the ellipses) and draw out the word *razor* until it almost hisses in my mouth.

TIP *Don't deliver your punch word indiscriminately. Antion suggests that you focus your attention on the person in your audience most likely to laugh. If you watch comedy clubs on television, you'll see professionals do exactly this. Why waste a good punch word on a sour puss? Antion also notes that by choosing someone who is likely to laugh, you increase your feeling of confidence as you deliver the line.*

5. **The arrangement of the elements didn't properly set up the joke.** Each piece of the humorous puzzle must build on the last and support the next. Have you ever constructed a catenary arch? In the St. Louis Science Center, they have one made of foam blocks that people can assemble to see how our beautiful Arch works. If any piece is missing, the arch will tumble. So it is with funny bits: each piece must be there for the structure to hold up. Take for example, the famous vaudeville joke:

Funny Man: "I met a man on the street who told me he hadn't had a bite in weeks."

Straight Man: "So what did you do?"

Funny Man: "I bit him."

It wouldn't work if the elements were scrambled or the rhythm was off:

Funny Man: "I met a guy the other day who was hungry . . . so I bit him."

See the difference the set-up makes?

6. **The audience "missed" your point.** This can happen for several reasons. Speakers who use clip-on microphones often turn their heads to the left or right, which makes it impossible for the microphone to pick up their voices. Wilde suggests that if you want to do humor, you stick to a hand-held mike. Michael Iapoce suggests that you lean into the microphone and *punch out* the key word. Whatever you do, make it clear to the audience that this is the crucial piece of information they've been waiting for.

In addition, you should pause for a second or two before you deliver your punch line. "The pause gives them time to visualize the verbal picture you've created, or simply to grasp the situation you've described," explains Iapoce. Wilde disagrees and says, "The punch line should be delivered in the same rhythm and the same cadence as the rest of the sentence." Listen to the master of the pause, Jack Benny. Benny's most famous bit was his response to a robber. The robber says, "Your money or your life." Jack Benny paused, then slowly responded, "I'm thinking!"

Similarly, your listeners may also miss your point if they are unfamiliar with a word, term, name, or concept that you use. For example, Mayfield struggled for years to use a funny bit about MENSA. Finally it dawned on him that most of the audience members couldn't quickly recall what MENSA was. He altered his joke to give more information. "What is the IQ requirement for MENSA anyway? I think you need an IQ of 140 to get in. I don't really know because my brother and I have a joint membership." Without patronizing the listeners, he subtly reminded them of what they needed to know to enjoy his humor.

7. **You didn't pause after the humorous bit long enough for the audience to react.** Use your face, and mug it up shamelessly. Use your voice to exaggerate the point. Here's a story I tell that could fall flat without my physicality and judicious timing: "The other day, my husband was feeling kind of romantic. We were standing in the kitchen discussing vacation spots. Finally, he hugged me and said, 'My favorite spot on earth is in your arms.' Then our son piped up and said, 'Why?'"

If you don't give the audience a chance to digest what is said and laugh about it after you deliver your punch line, you "step on the laugh." Since those on the comedy circuit live and die by the amount of laughter they generate, professional comedians pause for laughter and keep silent until it dies down. They often even mug it up while the laughter continues to keep the hilarity coming. Many amateur humorists tend to mumble through the punch line, fade on the punch word, and start talking while the audience is still building to the laugh.

TIP *To laugh or not to laugh at your jokes. That is the question. Experts generally agree you shouldn't. They prefer for you to stand there looking slightly stunned by the* *audience's reactions. However, both Liz Curtis Higgs and Carl Hurley laugh at themselves with gusto. Hurley's laugh—a high-pitched giggle that reminds one of Mozart in the movie* Amadeus—*is infectious enough to jump start an entire room into giggling along. By contrast, Ron Dentinger delivers his lines with a deadpan face and never cracks a giggle.*

So the answer is . . . try it both ways and see which way works best for you.

8. **The bit lacks enough exaggeration to make the punch word or punch line truly a surprise.** For me, creating outrageous characters with their own gestures and voices aids my set-up. I try to use this next story only after the audience has heard that I am from Vincennes, Indiana, the home of the "famous" watermelon festival. Knowing how tiny Vincennes is makes the bit much, much funnier.

> My sister, Margaret, and I bought tickets at the Metro station in Paris. Now Margaret had two years of French in high school and so did I, so between us we could speak just enough French to talk to the ticket taker. We got on the train and switched back to English. Next to us sat a man wearing a faded John Deere cap and a woman who was obviously his wife. Suddenly, the man nudged his wife, "Martha, Martha, isn't that what I was saying? They speak two languages here and they do it so well." Then he turned to Margaret and said—(and I really exaggerate his country accent, his slow and loud speech here)— "How long have you been speaking En-glish?" Margaret replied, "My whole life." (Then I pantomime the man slapping his hand on his knee.) "Martha, didn't I tell you? Didn't I tell you that's why they can talk two languages here so good. They start 'em early, Martha. Just like I said." Then he turned back to Margaret, "Who taught you to speak En-glish?" (And again, I draw out each word and say it loud with exaggerated enunciation.) "My parents," said Margaret. "Martha, Martha! They learn it at their parents'

knees. I told you!" He leaned in again, "Where do your parents live?" Margaret said, "Vincennes . . . Indiana." And Martha chirped, "Hey, that's where they have that watermelon festival! We live across the river in Olney!"

It works because I use the rule of threes (the man asks Margaret three questions), foreshadowing (you know Margaret isn't a French woman), exaggeration (he speaks overly loudly and in exaggerated tones the way most of us do when talking to foreigners), irony (he keeps talking about education and it is obvious that his own command of the English language is a bit shaky), and a call-back to an earlier piece (Vincennes being the home of the watermelon festival). The element of surprise is finding out Margaret's identity as an American and the crashing down of his theory that only Europeans learn two languages. By having Martha deliver the final words, I add a bit of spice because she has been the silent recipient of his superiority. (For those who are well-traveled, there is the bonus jolt of realizing that the Bois de Vincennes is a park very close to Paris.)

I act out the man, his wife, Margaret, and Martha, making each character distinctive. Margaret is a little confused, but polite and keeps her voice well-modulated. The man is the quintessential "ugly American," loud, aggressive, taking up a lot of space, and totally dominating. Then, Martha is friendly, excited, and unassuming. I asked myself how each of these people would sit, talk, and gesture. The resulting three characters add the spice!

By the way, the use of exaggeration and enunciation didn't come to me by accident. I once saw a terrific play called *The Foreigner* by Larry Shue, which turns on how silly we Americans are when we try to interact with someone from another country. When I create, I draw on every memory I have. As I pondered how curious this man's behavior was, I realized it rang a bell . . . and recalled *The Foreigner.*

You may have noticed that the humorous bit about Paris breaks a rule: It is long. However, it works because there is so much entertainment value along the way. Because the listener knows the John Deere cap man has made a mistake, the listener willingly devotes extra time to the story, wondering how this all will turn out.

The rule is: The longer the piece, the funnier it has to be. And, if it is long, the piece should entertain the audience on the way to the punch line.

HOW TO CREATE HUMOR

Just as stories can be created, so can humor. Once you identify a few patterns, you can build your own humor the same way people build a sundae at a self-serve dessert bar. Here are fifteen of my favorite humor potions.

1. **On a scale of . . .** Ask people to rate an experience by giving them funny definitions of 1 and 10. Ask your audiences, "Rate this on a scale of 1 to 10 with one being a root canal . . . without anesthesia."
2. **Top-ten list.** Borrow ideas from the best. One of them is certainly David Letterman. This works best when you customize it for the group you're speaking to. Ask the meeting planner to tell you the group's pet peeves and work together on it.
3. **Take it literally.** A whole world of literal humor exists when you quit taking the commonplace for granted. One day the students in an English as a Second Language class were buzzing like crazy. Then they asked the teacher, "If in America bigger is better, is a big jerk better than a small one?" Actually, that's not what they said at all. They were using descriptive names for body parts, but this is a family publication, so . . .
4. **Mistaken identity.** Here's one that can happen anytime, anywhere. Once, while sitting in a hotel waiting

for my ride, I called out to a young man, "Are you the taxi?" He responded, "No, ma'am, I'm the driver." Here's another: A man in the grocery store was stopped by a pretty young lady who struck up a conversation with him. "What nationality are you?" asked the pretty young thing. "I'm Lebanese," said the man. From behind a display of cleaning products, an older woman stepped out. "And I'm Mrs. Lebanese."

5. **Malapropism.** A misused word, or a word confused with another, is a malapropism. As long as the audience recognizes the intended meaning, these offer rich humor potential. For example, the phone rang and a man asked, "Is this the water titillation plant?" (He meant filtration.)

6. **Strange bedfellows.** By combining ideas that aren't usually considered together, you can create comedy. Here are a few examples: "This is my second marriage: I've been recycled." "Full-time speaker, full-time mother, and part-time blonde . . . " "I can be found at finer stores everywhere."

7. **How many people does it take to screw in a lightbulb?** Credit for this goes to Karyn Buxman, who allowed a government agency to brainstorm the answers to this one. She replaced *people* with *government workers*. You can do the same with any group from any industry. Just make sure they come up with the answers so you don't look like you are making fun of them.

8. **Wacky definitions.** Throw out your copy of *Webster's* and define or explain something in an offbeat way: "My dog Kevin is a Bichon Frise. For those of you who don't know what a Bichon Frise is, think of a very happy dust mop . . . with legs."

9. **Point up the absurdity.** Why do people hide their underwear under their other clothes when they strip at a doctor's office? I asked a nurse if everyone did this. She burst into gales of laughter. "We see every part of you and you hide your undies! What do you want us to think? That you didn't wear underwear into the office?"

So much of what we do is absurd that you can have a lot
of fun with this one.

10. **Make a comparison.** "He sank lower than the belly of
    a reptile." "She's about as much fun as vacuuming my
    carpet." Make an outrageous comparison and go for the
    chuckles.

11. **Pretend to be someone else.** David Knox can mimic
    almost as many people as Rich Little. During presenta-
    tions on sales, he becomes all sorts of folks, including
    John Wayne and Clint Eastwood. If you have a gift for
    mimicry, you can keep your audiences in stitches.

12. **Create a funny song.** In my presentations on life bal-
    ance, I have people sing, "No, no, no, I won't," to the
    tune of "Row, row, row, your boat." Rely on old familiar
    songs with well-known tunes to make this work.

13. **Share an unusual fact.** Not long ago, a survey done
    in Germany found that most German men would rather
    give up sex with their wives or girlfriends than give up
    their cars.

14. **Then add an observation.** "All I want to know is,
    what are those men driving?"

15. **Fracture a fairy tale.** "This morning my allergies
    make me feel like three of the seven dwarves: Sneezy,
    Sleazy, and Dopey. I guess I need to see Doc."

PLAY OFF YOUR PERSONA

If you know how others perceive you, you can play off that
persona and enjoy the laughs. Bubba Bechtol portrays himself
as a "good ole boy," a bit baffled by the ultrasophistication all
around him. Nancy Nix-Rice teases that "when people hear
how young my children are they think I'm a very worn-out
looking young mom. The truth is, I didn't get started having
my family until late in life, and I'm really a very well-pre-
served old mom, thank you."

When you read the audience's minds, you can create
humor by disavowing them of their misconceptions about

you. You can get away with this because you didn't try to trick them . . . they fooled themselves.

ABOUT THE HECKLERS . . .

Don't worry too much about hecklers. As long as your humor supports your message, you will find that few people in business settings want to identify themselves to their peers and supervisors by giving you a hard time.

Mayfield suggests ignoring hecklers for as long as possible. Use your body to block the heckler from your line of sight and keep on presenting if the noise level of the heckler isn't too great. If the heckling persists, call for a break—or assign the audience a task to work on with partners—and ask the meeting planner to help you decide how best to handle the situation.

Never, ever make fun of a heckler. This works in night club audiences because the group does not know each other. Groups who work together or belong to the same organization are different. When the heckler is one of their own, the group will rally around the offender faster than you can say, "That's all, folks."

DON'T FORGET TO PRACTICE

Now that you have the basics of humor and you've developed your bits, don't overlook the crucial element: Practice. As Antion says, "You must become so familiar with the material that you can present it in what appears to be a spontaneous unrehearsed fashion." Nothing ruins good comedy more than muffing your punch line or forgetting that perfect punch word. With practice comes confidence. You can relax and enjoy yourself because you know what's coming next.

As Antion says, "Practicing bits and stories is really great because you can do it in little pieces of throwaway time in the shower or in the car." Patricia Fripp practices everywhere she goes, in airports and while walking.

Speaker Mark Sanborn has commented, "How can you improve your delivery unless you practice?" Sanborn sets aside time daily to work on how he delivers his presentations, which helps explain why he is regarded as one of the most polished presenters on the platform today.

SUMMARY

Humor is all around you. In this chapter, we looked at why humor occasionally falls flat. We showed ways you can develop humor and explained the value of playing off your persona. Finally, we explored methods for dealing with hecklers, and we emphasized the need to practice your humorous delivery.

EXERCISES

1. Time a humorous story you have been working on. Now try to cut the length of the story to 15 seconds.
2. Listen to another person tell a humorous story. Is the punch line or punch word at the end? Can you identify the punch line or punch word?
3. Note the punch line or punch word in one of your own humorous stories. Change it so that it uses hard consonants.
4. Watch other speakers or classmates tell a humorous piece. Use the list of ideas covered in the section Failings of Would-Be Humorists (on page 205) to improve the piece.
5. Choose one idea from the list in the section How to Create Humor (on page 210) and work to create humor.
6. Discuss the concept of persona and how you can use it to be funnier.

Bibliography

Allen, Steve. *How to Be Funny.* New York: McGraw-Hill, 1987.

Allen, Steve. *How to Make a Speech.* New York: McGraw-Hill, 1986.

The American Heritage Dictionary. Boston: Houghton Mifflin, 1985.

Antion, Tom. *Wake 'Em Up.* Landover Hills, MD: Anchor Publishing and Creative Training Techniques, Minneapolis, 1997.

Barker, Joel Arthur. *Future Edge.* New York: William Morrow, 1992.

Bates, Roger. *How to Be Funnier.* Minneapolis, MN: Trafton, 1995.

Bateson, Mary Catherine. *With a Daughter's Eye,* New York: HarperPerennial, 1994.

Bedrosian, Maggie. *Speak Like a Pro.* Rockville, MD: BCI Press, 1994.

Bennett, William J. *The Children's Book of Virtues.* New York: Simon & Schuster, 1995.

Berman, Philip, & Connie Goldman. *The Ageless Spirit.* New York: Ballantine Books, 1992.

Borysenko, Joan. *Fire in the Soul.* New York: Warner, 1993.

Bowman, Sharon. *Presenting with Pizzazz! Terrific Tips for Topnotch Trainers!* New York: Glenbrook, NV: Bowperson, 1997.

Boyd, Lorrie, Lola Gillebaard, Stewart Lerner, & Jeanne Lerner. *Change Your Life with Humor.* Long Beach, CA: ADD/WRITE, 1993.

Cahill, Thomas. *How the Irish Saved Civilization: The Untold Story of Ireland's Heroic Role from the Fall of Rome to the Rise of Medieval Europe.* New York: Anchor, 1995.

Cameron, Julia. *The Artist's Way.* New York: Jeremy P. Tarcher/Putnam, 1992.

Capote, Truman. *In Cold Blood.* New York: Random House, 1965.

Chapman, Joyce. *Journaling for Joy.* Van Nuys, CA: Newcastle, 1991.

Davis, Donald. *Telling Your Own Stories.* Little Rock, AR: August House, 1993.

Dowling, Ellen. *The Standup Trainer.* Alexandria, VA: ASTD, and Minneapolis, MN: Creative Training Techniques, 1995.

Franklin, Jon. *Writing for Story.* New York: Atheneum, 1986.

Fripp, Patricia. *Get What You Want.* Costa Mesa, CA: H.D.L., 1988.

George, Elizabeth. *For the Sake of Elena.* New York: Bantam, 1992.

Glazov, Sheila. *Princess Shayna's Invisible Visible Gift.* Tower Lakes, IL: Peridot Productions, 1997.

Goldberg, Natalie. *Writing Down the Bones.* Boston: Shambhala, 1986.

Goodman, Gerald R., & Glen Esterly. *The Talk Book: The Intimate Science of Communicating in Close Relationships.* Emmaus, PA: Rodale, 1988.

Grun, Bernard. *The Timetables of History.* New York: Simon & Schuster, 1991.

Hansen, Mark Victor, & Jack Canfield. *Chicken Soup for the Soul.* Deerfield Beach, Florida, 1993; *Chicken Soup for the Soul at Work.* Deerfield Beach, FL: Health Communications, 1996.

Harrison, Jim. *The Legends of the Fall.* Thorndike, ME: Thorndike Press, 1979.

Hawken, Paul. *Growing a Business.* New York: Simon & Schuster, 1987.

Helmbold, F. Wilbur. *Tracing Your Ancestry Logbook*. Birmingham, AL: Oxmoor, 1976.

Humes, James C. *Standing Ovation*. New York: Harper & Row, 1988.

Hyatt, Carole. *The Woman's New Selling Game*. New York: McGraw-Hill, 1997.

Klepper, Michael. *I'd Rather Die Than Give a Speech*. Burr Ridge, IL: Irwin Professional, 1994.

Kushner, Malcolm. *The Light Touch*. New York: Simon & Schuster, 1991.

L'Engle, Madeleine. *The Summer of the Great-Grandmother*. New York: HarperCollins, 1977.

Livo, Norma J., & Sandra A. Rietz. *Storytelling: Process & Practice*. Littleton, CO: Libraries Limited, 1987.

Moussaieff Masson, Jeffrey, & Susan McCarthy. *When Elephants Weep*. New York: Delacorte, 1995.

Mohr, Franz. *My Life with the Great Pianists*. Grand Rapids, MI: Baker Book House, 1992.

Nix-Rice, Nancy. *Looking Good: A Comprehensive Guide to Wardrobe Planning, Color and Personal Style Development*. Portland, OR: Palmer/Pletsch, 1996.

Paulson, Terry. *Making Humor Work*. Menlo Park, CA: Crisp, 1989.

Paulson, Terry. *They Shoot Managers Don't They?* Berkeley, CA: Ten Speed, 1991.

Pearson, Carol S. *The Hero Within*. San Francisco: Harper & Row, 1989.

Perez, Rosita. *The Music Is You*. Granville, OH: Knox, 1994.

Rivers, Joan. *Enter Talking*. New York: Delacorte Press, 1986.

Robertson, Jeanne Swanner. *Mayberry Humor Across the USA*. Houston, TX: Rich, 1995.

Robinson, Grady Jim.*The Substance, Sizzle, and Soul of Speaking* (audio album). St. Louis, MI: Robinson & Robinson, 1993.

Rhyne, Nancy. *Tales of the South Carolina Low Country*. Winston-Salem, NC: Blair, 1982.

Rhyne, Nancy. *More Tales of the South Carolina Low Country*. Winston-Salem, NC: Blair, 1984.

Schank, Roger C. *Tell Me a Story.* New York: Scribner's, 1990.

Shedlock, Marie L. *The Art of the Story-Teller.* Mineola, NY: Dover, 1951.

Snow, Kimberley. *Writing Yourself Home: A Woman's Guided Journey of Self Discovery.* Berkeley, CA: Conari Press, 1992.

Stack, Jack. *The Great Game of Business.* New York: Currency Doubleday, 1992.

St. Louis Post-Dispatch. "Bertram Minkin, 45: Writer and Professional Storyteller," August 20, 1996.

Thomas, Frank P. *How to Write the Story of Your Life.* Cincinnati, OH: Writers Digest Books, 1984.

Trelease, Jim.*The Read-Aloud Book.* New York: Penguin, 1995.

Ueland, Brenda. *If You Want to Write.* St. Paul, MN: Graywolf, 1987.

Varga, Mari Pat. *Great Openings and Closing: Launch and Land Your Presentations with Punch, Power, and Pizazz.* Mission, KS: SkillPath, 1996.

Waite, Arthur Edward. *Pictoral Key to the Tarot.* New York: Causeway, 1973.

Walters, Lilly. *When to Say When . . . You're Dying on the Platform.* New York: McGraw-Hill, 1995.

Walters, Lilly, & Dottie, Walters. *Speak and Grow Rich.* Englewood Cliffs, NJ: Prentice-Hall, 1989.

Welty, Eudora. *One Writer's Beginnings.* Cambridge, MA: Harvard University Press, 1984.

Wilson, Frank R. *Tone Deaf and All Thumbs?* New York: Viking, 1986.

Zinsser, William. *Writing to Learn.* New York: Harper & Row, 1988.

Zipes, Jack. *Creative Storytelling: Building Community, Changing Lives.* New York: Routledge, 1995.

About Toastmasters International

If the thought of public speaking is enough to stop you dead in your tracks, it may have the same effect on your career.

While surveys report that public speaking is one of people's most dreaded fears, the fact remains that the inability to effectively deliver a clear thought in front of others can spell doom for professional progress. The person with strong communication skills has a clear advantage over tongue-tied colleagues—especially in a competitive job market.

Toastmasters International, a nonprofit educational organization, helps people conquer their pre-speech jitters. From one club started in Santa Ana, California, in 1924, the organization now has more than 170,000 members in 8,300 clubs in 62 countries.

How Does It Work?

A Toastmasters club is a "learn by doing" workshop in which men and women hone their communication and leadership skills in a friendly, supportive atmosphere. A typical club has 20 members who meet weekly or biweekly to practice public speaking techniques. Members, who pay approximately $35 in dues twice a year, learn by progressing through a series of 10 speaking assignments and being evaluated on their performance by their fellow club members. When finished with the basic speech manual, members can select from among 14 advanced programs that are geared toward specific career needs. Members also have the opportunity to develop and practice leadership skills by working in the High Performance Leadership Program.

Besides taking turns to deliver prepared speeches and evaluate those of other members, Toastmasters give impromptu talks on assigned topics, usually related to current events. They also develop listening skills, conduct meetings, learn parliamentary procedure and gain leadership experience by serving as club officers. But most importantly, they develop self-confidence from accomplishing what many once thought impossible.

The benefits of Toastmasters' proven and simple learning formula has not been lost on the thousands of corporations that sponsor in-house Toastmasters clubs as cost-efficient means of satisfying their employees' needs for communication training. Toastmasters clubs can be found in the U.S. Senate and the House of Representatives, as well as in a variety of community organizations, prisons, universities, hospitals, military bases, and churches.

How to Get Started

Most cities in North America have several Toastmasters clubs that meet at different times and locations during the week. If you are interested in forming or joining a club, call (714) 858-8255. For a listing of local clubs, call (800) WE-SPEAK, or write Toastmasters International, PO Box 9052, Mission Viejo, California 92690, USA. You can also visit our website at http://www.toastmasters.org.

As the leading organization devoted to teaching public speaking skills, we are devoted to helping you become more effective in your career and daily life.

Terrence J. McCann
Executive Director, Toastmasters International

Allyn & Bacon Order Form
The **Essence of Public Speaking** Series

Now you can order the rest of the books in the series — only $12.00 each!

Available Now!

__*Speaking for Profit and Pleasure: Making the Platform Work for You,*
by William D. Thompson, Order #T70262

__*Speaking Your Way to the Top: Making Powerful Business Presentations,*
by Marjorie Brody, Order # T68142

__*TechEdge: Using Computers to Present and Persuade,*
by William J. Ringle, Order #T73050

__*Using Stories and Humor—Grab Your Audience,*
by Joanna Slan, Order # T68936

__*Writing Great Speeches: Professional Techniques You Can Use,*
by Alan Perlman, Order # T73001

Available Fall 1998*

__*Adapting Your Speech to Every Audience,*
by Shirley E. Nice, Order # T70254

__*Choosing Powerful Words,* by Ronald H. Carpenter, Order # T71245

__*Delivering Dynamic Presentations,* by Ralph Hillman, Order # T68100

__*Involving Your Audience—Make it Active,*
by Karen E. Lawson, Order # T68118

__*Motivating Your Audience,* by Hanoch McCarty, Order # T68944

* Prices and titles subject to change

Name: _____

Address:_____

City: _____State: _____Zip:_____

Phone: _____E-mail: _____

__Charge my   __AMEX __VISA __Mastercard ___Discover

Credit Card # _____ Exp. Date_____

__Check __Money Order *Prepay by check or money order for free shipping and handling*

To place an order:

MAIL:
Allyn & Bacon Publishers
111 10th Street
Des Moines, IA 50309

CALL toll-free: 1-800-278-3525
FAX: 1-515-284-2607
WEBSITE: www.abacon.com

MPG002   B1270A1-1